Anonymus

The Irish Ecclesiastical Record

Volume 4, No. 9, 1868

Anonymus

The Irish Ecclesiastical Record
Volume 4, No. 9, 1868

ISBN/EAN: 9783741199936

Manufactured in Europe, USA, Canada, Australia, Japa

Cover: Foto ©Thomas Meinert / pixelio.de

Manufactured and distributed by brebook publishing software
(www.brebook.com)

Anonymus

The Irish Ecclesiastical Record

SINGLE COPY, EIGHT PENCE; BY POST, NINE PENCE.

VOL. IV.

No. IX.

THE IRISH

ECCLESIASTICAL RECORD:

A Monthly Journal.

CONDUCTED BY A SOCIETY OF CLERGYMEN,

UNDER EPISCOPAL SANCTION.

No. XLV. JUNE, 1868.

"Ut Christiani ita et Romani sitis".

" As you are children of Christ, so be you children of Rome".

Ex Dictis S. Patricii, Book of Armagh, fol. 9.

DUBLIN:

JOHN F. FOWLER, 3 CROW STREET.

PER ANNUM, SIX SHILLINGS; BY POST, SEVEN SHILLINGS.

THE IRISH
ECCLESIASTICAL RECORD.

JUNE, 1868.

CONTENTS.

	Page.
I. Inscribed Stones of Killeen Cormac, County Kildare,	431
II. University Education in Ireland,	432
III. Subterranean Rome,	449
IV. Remarks on the Address presented to the Queen by the Irish Protestant Bishops,	457
V. Documents :—	
1. Address of the St. Peter's Pence Central Committee, Dublin, to His Holiness, transmitting the names of the contributors to the special Collection, 1st February, 1868,	461
2. Letter of our Most Holy Father to the President and Secretaries of the Peter's Pence Association, in reply to the above Address,	463
3. Letter of the Cardinal Prefect of Propaganda to the Cardinal Archbishop of Dublin, on Mixed Schools,	463
VI. Notice of Book:—Notes on the Rubrics of the Roman Ritual,	468

Imprimatur,

✠ PAULUS CARDINALIS CULLEN,
Archiepiscopus Dubliniensis.

Dublin, Maii 30, 1868.

Communications to the Editors, and books for review, should be addressed to the care of Mr. J. F. Fowler, 3 Crow Street, Dublin.

THE IRISH
ECCLESIASTICAL RECORD.

JUNE, 1868.

INSCRIBED STONES OF KILLEEN CORMAC, COUNTY KILDARE.

AN ESSAY TO IDENTIFY THAT CHURCH WITH THE CELL FINE OF PALLADIUS.

THE cemetery of Killeen Cormac lies about three miles to the south-west of Dunlavan, midway between that town and the village of Ballytore. It is situated in the lands of Colbinstown, in a detached portion of the parish of Davidstown, in the barony of East Narragh and Reban, county Kildare. This very interesting and very ancient cemetery lies in a valley of the most picturesque character, traversed by the river Griese, separating in this spot Wicklow from Kildare, and the diocese of Leighlin from that of Glendalough. Its surface is covered with many insulated mounds or eskars, still retaining their ancient names, which, as they are connected with the history of the locality, will be here described. On the left bank of the Griese is a long eskar, called Bullock Hill. On the opposite bank is another of oval form called, perhaps by contrast, Cnoc Bunnion.[1] Beyond this is another elevation, the highest of the group, on the top of which is a well preserved moat or rath of large proportions; by its base runs a rivulet called the Scrughan (i.e. streamlet), which joins the Griese in the vicinity. This rath is called Rathounbeg.[2] Between this mound and Cnoc Bunnion is an eskar of oval shape, measuring 230 paces in circumference, its major axis lying nearly east and west; the summit of its western end, where its elevation is greatest, is

---

[1] bunian, is feminine; bo, gen. boin, a cow.
[2] ꞃáꞇ abhain beg, i.e. the rath of the little brook.

fashioned into a rath or mound, the sides of which show the remains of three terraces. The first on the ground line seems to have enclosed the whole eskar. The remains of the second and third terraces are still to be traced around the moat on its western side. The whole hill is now occupied by graves, and on the top of the moat there is a square depression which was most probably the site of the ancient church. A great quantity of large stones lie about, and plainly indicate the former existence of some structure of primitive design and architecture. The terraces are now in a very ruinous state, but sufficient indications remain to disclose their original design and mode of construction. On the south-east the middle terrace is well preserved: it is supported by large flat stones set against the bank they sustain, so that before these terraces were dilapidated, the entire structure, crowned by a massive building, must have had an imposing appearance, which may be realized from the immense stones,—fragments of very rude and ancient crosses of coarse granite, pillar stones of ponderous appearance and size, which were placed at intervals around the lowest terrace, together with the remains of their Cyclopean walls—all give to Killeen Cormac an appearance of antiquity which it is extremely difficult to describe.

It has been suggested that Killeen Cormac was in the pre-Christian period used as a place of pagan sepulchre. Its very peculiar construction and the indications of a sepulchral chamber within the moat, with passages to the terraces such as are to be found in similar structures at New Grange on the Boyne, and in other localities, give an air of certainty to the suggestion, which is well sustained by the appearance of a stone on the south side of the mound about three feet high, fixed in the wall of the middle terrace. It seems to be one of the jambs of a door to the entrance leading from the central cave. The side of this stone is grooved, the opposite jamb was likely hollowed in the same manner to receive a thinner flag to close the exterior entrance. Killeen Cormac has the reputation of being full of rats, as well as of being the oldest cemetery in the whole country. These animals are up to this time the only explorers of the subterranean galleries under the mound, since they were closed up to preserve the remains of some pagan hero of the earliest dawn of history. The most recent fact connected with this cemetery is, that about the year 1830 a stone wall was built around its area, some trees were then planted which add a phase of beauty peculiarly their own, while their shadows give a dim religious light in harmony with the venerable relics of antiquity of which they are the guardians.

Within the enclosure, and on the sides of the ruined terraces, are some inscribed pillar stones, with Latin and Ogham inscriptions, and some very curious incised figures, the description of which is reserved for notice at the close of this paper.

At the side of the mound, some paces from the entrance, is one pillar stone, now about three feet above the surface, on the top of which is an indentation resembling the trace of a hound's paw, as if impressed on a soft surface. Excavations made around it did not reveal any features worth describing. A very curious legend, founded indeed on historical facts, is told concerning this stone, with a view, perhaps, to account for the name Cormac being affixed to the locality. The tradition of the neighbourhood says that the pillar stone marks the grave of a Cormac, king of Munster. It states that he was carried to this cemetery for sepulture by a team of bullocks, which were allowed to follow their own instincts, a mode of settling disputes regarding sepulture not uncommon among the ancient Irish. Such was employed in selecting the final resting place of St. Patrick. We find it also in the life of St. Abban Mac Ua Cormaic,[1] which may have been suggested by the Scriptural precedent of sending home the Ark of the Covenant by the Philistines to Judea.[2] This tradition, though unable to state the period or circumstances of King Cormac's death, avers that he was carried from a long distance through Ballynure from Timolin, in the county Kildare, and when the team reached that part of Ballymore now known as "the Doon", the exhausted bullocks, in the eagerness of their thirst, pawed the earth, and that a stream of water issued forth. Another version states that the teamster stuck his goad into the ground, whereupon gushed up a bubbling fountain, which is still to be found near the roadside, and is used as a watering-place for the kine pasturing on the fertile heights at the Doon of Ballynure. The bullocks having satisfied their thirst, journeyed on till they came to the elevation now called Bullock Hill, beside the Griese, opposite to Killeen Cormac. Here they halted, and refused to proceed farther, from which it appeared that Killeen was to be the last resting place of the king. The bullocks having done their part, returned homewards across the marsh, and were engulphed in the waters of the Griese. In this instance also this legend agrees with the account related by Colgan in the *Life of St. Abban.* Another version of this legend, but more confused, places a hound on the team, which, when it stopped at Bullock Hill, jumped over to the cemetery, and left the impression of its paw on the pillar stone, thus marking the grave of Cormac; while another story represents this hound as jumping from the summit of Knockadhow, still more remote

[1] St. Abban Mac Ua Cormaic, born circa 430, was seventh in descent from Cormac Caech, son of Cucorb, K. L., and different from St. Abban of Maghairnuidhe, who was born A D. 520. V. *dissertation. Bol*, Oct. 27, p. 274. [2] Vide I. *Kings*, vi.

from the cemetery. These latter legends look like an interpretation from one more ancient concerning the hounds of Cuglos (son of Donndesa, King of Leinster), who was master of the hounds to Ederscoel, the great king of Erin, slain by Nuadha Neacht at Aillin,[1] A.M. 5089. From Cuglos, Baltinglass takes its name. His dogs hunted a wild boar from Tara to the Hill of Uske, where they left the marks of their paws on the stones of a druidical circle crowning its summit. The same traces are to be found on some rocks at Manger, near Rathbran. While pursuing their game up the hill over Beallach Dubhthaire, the ancient name of Baltinglass, Cuglos with his dogs, blinded by the mist and fog, chased their game into a cave on the summit of the mountain, and being there lost, his memory was perpetuated by giving his name[2] to the scene of his untimely fate. A similar story of King Arthur's hounds is told in the Irish version of Nennius. *I. A. Soc. Tracts,* p. 117.

About six years ago, the huntsmen and dogs of the Kildare Club were lost for some time in the fogs and mists of these mountains, and would only need the sacred poet to give a colouring of romance to their trackless wanderings, and clothe their exploits with a legendary interest.

As these accounts rest on historic grounds, investigations were made to discover who this king of Munster might be. Cormac Mac Cullinen, who fell at Ballachmoon, in Moyailbe,[3] A.D. 903, might have been the king of Munster sought for; but ancient authorities assert that he was buried at Castledermot. Keating in his account of the battle of Balleachmoon, states that

---

[1] Now Knockaulin, near old Kilcullen, county Kildare. The ruins of a deep circular entrenchment enclosing many acres in extent, attest the ancient magnificence and importance of this Leinster palace. It had its name from Aillinn, daughter of Lugaidh, son of Fergus Fairge, king of Leinster, at the close of the first century.—*Dinn Sencus,* fol. 193, a. b.

[2] A cave existed on Baltinglass hill till recent times. Quarrying operations on the face of the cliff overhanging it have almost obliterated its remains. On the summit of the hill is a large cairn called Rathcoran. On its northern slope is a smaller one called Rathnagree. Under these caissels are likely artificial caves. The lost tale of the chase of Cuglos might reveal something of interest in their history. Vide O'Curry's *Lectures,* app. p. 586, n. 145. The legend as told among the old natives of the neighbourhood is embodied in this paper. In mediæval documents the name is spelled Balkynglas, which approaches nearer the correct form of the ancient name.

[3] Moyailbe, the name of a plain in the northern portion of the modern county Carlow. It got its name from a famous hound called Ailbhe, belonging to Mac Mac Datho, king of Leinster in the first century. Dr. O'Donovan says that Ballachmoon, between Carlow and Castledermot, was the scene of this battle. There are no traditions of it in that locality. While at Ballymoon east of Leighlin Bridge there are traditions connected with Cormac Mac Culinan, the stone on which he was decapitated is still shown there. The text of Keating's *Irish History* seems to point to that very place, and the notice of this battle in the *Book of Leinster* makes Cormac pass over the hills of Hy Mairge to Leighlin Bridge, and march directly east of the Barrow.

Cormac having a presentiment of his impending fate, desired to be buried in Desert Diarmit (Castledermot), where rested the remains of its abbot, Snegdus, who died A.D. 888. He was the tutor and guardian of Cormac's early youth, and with him he wished his remains to lie, in case they could not be conveyed to Cluain Uamha (Cloyne). There was, however, in the same fatal field of Ballachmoon another Cormac, Cormac Mac Mothla, prince or regulus of the Decies of Munster.[1] All historical authorities give his name among the slain, having fallen while commanding the left wing of the Munster army. His death is, however, recorded in the *Chronicon Scotorum* ten years later, but the circumstantial evidence of other writers must outweigh its authority in this instance. Was he the Cormac of the legend in question? Local tradition could not solve this difficulty, but subsequent information, given by a gentleman whose father was a repertory of the traditions of the locality, stated that the personage whose name was connected with Killeen, was Cormac Mac Melia, king of Munster, thus adding another link to the chain of historical facts connected with the history of the battle of Ballachmoon. Though it appears that Cormac Mac Cullinan had obvious reasons for selecting Desert Diarmid as his last resting place, that church may not have had the same attractions for his namesake of the Desies. It may be supposed he made arrangements of this nature before the fate of the battle decided his lot, or there may have been a contention between rival communities[2] (as often happened in these, as well as in subsequent times) for the honour and emolument of giving sepulture to the remains of a veteran warrior; or it may be that Cormac Mac Mothlas's adherents, following an ancient precedent, may have allowed animal instinct to settle a dispute which the obstinacy or cupidity

---

[1] The *Annals of the Four Masters* also represent Cormac Mac Mothla in 915 as slaying Mailruanadh, tanist of the Deisi. In 917 his death is again recorded. Mistakes and double entries sometimes occur in these annals.

[2] *e.g.* The contention of the monks of Bective and the canons of St. Thomas's Abbey, Dublin, concerning the right to possess the remains of Sir Hugh De Lacy, slain at Durrow, 1186. This suit was terminated only in 1205, the canons being the victors. Vide *A. F. M.* sub annis, *Lodge*, vol. vi. p. 140. See also the lives of SS. Gall and Genebern. Also the dispute between the Cistercian monks of Assaroe concerning the right to give sepulture to the body of Murrough O'Brien, the fourth baron of Inchiquin, who was slain at a ford on the river Erne, July 29, 1597. Vide *Lodge*, vol ii. p. 46, *A. F. M.* sub ann. This custom has continued up to very recent times. In the year 1772 a very formidable dispute arose among the parishioners of Kells and Kilmoganny in the county Kilkenny. Their pastor, the Rev. Richard Shee (a relative of Dr. Patrick Shee, born 1664, appointed bishop of Ossory, July 28, 1731, died 1736), died July 17, 1772. He was buried with his parents in Sloncarty, near Kells. The Killamorey folk came at night, disinterred the body, and brought it to rest in their ancient cemetery of Killamorey, where it did not long remain, for the people of Kells, with his family, came and took away the remains and laid them in their first grave, filling it up with large rocks and stones to prevent any further attempts at removal.

of rival interests could not have otherwise arranged. Another reason, perhaps the strongest, is that Killeen had then, and for centuries before, the affix *Cormac*, as will appear further on, which probably marked out that cemetery as the last resting place of another Cormac, whose name might be considered as suggestive of the selection. The legend of the bullocks belongs to an earlier time, and is to be referred to the account given by Colgan (*Ac. SS. Hib. Martii*, cap. xlvii.) of the dispute concerning the place of sepulture of the body of St. Abban Mac Ua Cormaic. In the appendix to this life are enumerated more than sixty of the name, who were eminent in sanctity, among them is mentioned, Cormac Mac Ua Lethan, abbot of Durmagh,[1] who met with a tragical fate, being devoured by wolves in this locality. Thus far the traditions, which as may be seen, are of some value in a historical point of view. There is, however, an authority to show that the name of *Cormac*[2] was affixed to this cemetery and the surrounding country centuries before any of the events alluded to. It would appear from the *Book of Lecan*, fol. 95 a,

[1] A bishop Cormac Ua Lethan, who died 865, can't be the person referred to by St. Columba. Vide his *Life* by Adamnan, ed. Dr. Reeves add notes, p. 273:

> "Sharply hast thou attacked me, O Memonian,
> O Cormac of memorable sense.
> Wolves shall eat thy body
> For this deed without any mercy".

[2] It would appear from this extract kindly supplied by Mr. William M. Hennessy, that the territory in which Killeen Cormac is situated belonged to a branch of the tribe of Messincorb, called the Ui Cormaic, or Fine Cormaic, whose possessions with those of their correlatives are thus minutely described:

"ice ranoa h. ngabla ocur h. Copmaic La Laignib .i. na ngebche h. ngabla fine uili, ocur Cuchpaigi, ocur h. gabla paipeno, oca ach culcingeo co oub achaib maircen, otha glair Chpichi i Cluanaib co uavo fri Laigir, co clanocair, co hach Leathnocht oc Sleibcib, co ceic in urci fri huib mbaipnchi ocur anangebchi. h. chpena ocur h. Chuircc ir La .h. Chopmaic uili. ir oib Abban mac .h. Copmaic. ir uaoib machaip Cholum mic Cpimchainn .i. mincloch ingen Cenanoain, mic Ceri, mic Lugoach, mic Labpaoa. ir oib Copmaic in oa Sinell .i. Sinell mac Cenanoain mic macha, mic Chpuaich, mic Ouilgi, mic Imchaoa, mic bpolaig, mic Lugoach, mic Lubpaoa; ocur Sinell rean mac Copcpain, mic epc, mic Chipuaich, mic Ouilgi, ocur apaile".

" These are the divisions of Ui Gabhla and Ui Cormaic in Leinster, viz., where the Ui Gabhla all are found, and Cuthraighi and Ui Gabhla of Rairend (Mullach Reelan) ; from Ath-Culchinged to the Black Fords of Maisten (Mullachmast) ; from Glass[1] Crichi in Cluana[2] to Uado toward Laighis (Leix), to Clanties[3], to Ath-Leathnocht at Sleibhti (Sletty), until it goes into Usci (hill of Usk), towards Ui Bairchi ; and wherever are found[4] Ui Threna, and Ui Chuirc, all belongs to Ui Cormaic. Of them is Abban Mac Ui Cormaic. From them was the mother of Colum mac Crimthann,[5] viz. Mincloth, daughter of Cenanan . . . . . Of the Ui Cormaic are the two Sinells, viz., Sinell son of Cenanan . . . . . and old Sinell, son of Corcran, etc".

---

[1] The river Griese, i.e. the boundary stream. [2] Cluana, the plain around Killeen.
[3] Probably Clooney, near Athy. [4] O'Treanor, O'Quirk, or Mac Guirke, O'Cormac.
[5] Abbot of Tir-da-Glas (Terryglas), obit. 13th Dec. 552. [6] Sinnell senior, obit. 544, he was eighth in descent from Cucorb, K. L. V. *Trias. Th.* b. 18.

that the territory in which it is situated belonged to a correlative tribe of the Dalmessin-Corb, known as the Ua Cormaic, Dalcormaic, and Fine Cormaic, i.e. the descendants of the tribes of Cormaic. Their ancestor, Cormaic Caech, or Luscus, was son of Cucorb, king of Leinster, towards the close of the century before the Christian era, whence the name of the church and cemetery, Cell Fine Cormaic, i.e. the church of the tribes of Cormaic. In the accounts of the mission of Palladius to the Irish, A.D. 431, and of the churches erected by him, three are mentioned by him, two of which are identified with Tig-Roney and Donard, in the county Wicklow. As to the third church, called in the various lives of St. Patrick, *Cell Fine*, in the *Vita Quarta Ecclesia Finte*, which may be, as Colgan suggests, for *Fin-tech*, i.e Aedes Fine, there has been hitherto no attempt at identification. The passage in the *Book of Lecan*, just referred to, may perhaps give a clue to the identification of the Cell Fine, or Ecclesia Finte, of the writers of the acts of Palladius and St. Patrick, as it is admitted that Palladius traversed the mountainous regions of Hy-Garrcon to Donard, almost at its extreme western limits. Doubtless the sunny plains of Mid-Leinster, extending to the distant horizon, met his delighted eyes as he descended the western slopes of the Wicklow hills—a land of promise unfolded before him, more fruitful in soil, its tribes perhaps less hostile to his exertions, tempted him to advance even a little farther inland than historians testify. Hy-Garrcon then extended probably to the banks of the river Griese, " the boundary stream". Palladius having imbued " The Tribes" of Mid-Leinster with the saving truths of Christianity, dedicated to the service of the God of Heaven the scene of their pagan superstition, erecting there a church, which seems to be the one he loved most, placing there for safe keeping, and as a pledge of his zeal and gratitude, his writing materials, the relics brought from the tombs of the apostles, and the volume of the Holy Scripture presented to him by Pope Celestine.

The identification of this church with the Cell Fine of the Acta, will be still further verified by an examination of the very curious and venerable relics of the earliest Christian antiquity still happily preserved there. Among these are three monuments of a most archaic character, coeval with the earliest dawn of Christianity in Ireland, two of them unique in their kind. The accompanying woodcuts, accurately made from the rubbings taken by the writer on a scale of one inch to the foot, will make their description more intelligible. No. 1 is of coarse green stone, very rough and much weather worn; an Ogham inscription is carried up the two sides and top. It belongs to a class of monuments not quite so rare, having, however, an

interest peculiarly their own, proving, as they do, the use of letters among the pre-Christian Celts. The inscription
reads (Coirthe): MAQI
DDECEDA, MAQI MA
RIN[1] i.e. the pillar stone of
the son of Deœdda, the son
of Marin. Who these per-
sonages were it is impossible
to discover; the names are,
however, Celtic, cognate
with Cadoo, Catan, Keddan,
etc. Marin represents Mui-
rige, Moregan, Morgan. At
Penros Slygwy, in Anglesea,
a stone belonging to the end
of the sixth century bears
this inscription: "HIC IA-
CIT MACCVDECCETI".
It is described in the *Archaeo-
logia Cambrensis*, vol. vii., 3
series, p. 296. The similarity
of the names of the persons
commemorated on this as well
as on the Killeen Ogham is
very striking, and affords a
proof of the intercourse
existing between the Welsh
and the early Irish Christians. On the plateau on

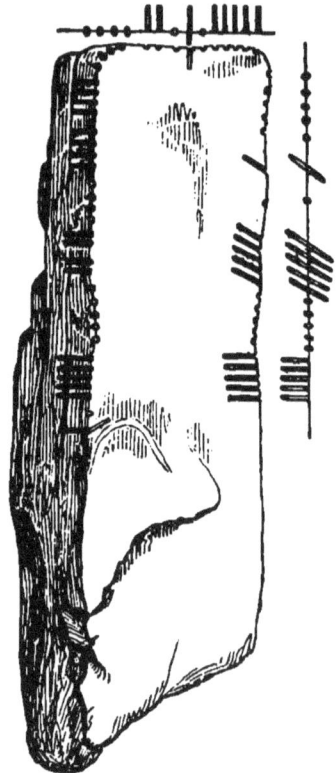

No. I.

the east side is an oblong rough flag-like uninscribed stone,
standing three feet nine inches over the ground and about two
feet wide. A plain cross, twenty-two inches long by fifteen in
the transverse arms, is incised on its face in wide shallow lines.
Some slabs of this character are to be found in Dunboyke
and Kilranelagh, and, likely, belong to a later period of Celtic
art.

No. 2, on the left of the modern entrance, is a block of green
stone, partially stratified, measuring in length six feet five inches,
the upper surface at the top ten inches wide, and at the base
eight inches; the side at the top eleven inches deep by fourteen
inches at the base. This pillar, on its top surface, bears a faintly
incised bust, which appears to represent the Redeemer, in a
style of art so very archaic that any example of similar work-

---

[1] The reading of Samuel Ferguson, Esq., LL.D., M. R. I. A.

manship is scarcely to be found in these islands. On the same side, but near the middle, and close to the edge or orris of this stone, three incised strokes or scores exist, as if a commencement had been made for an inscription in the Ogham character. On the side of the stone, under these scores, is a mark of the stratification, across which is cut a single score, looking, as it now stands, like a cross, being probably another attempt at an Ogham inscription.

The pillar stone, No. 3, is of the same material, but of more irregular outlines. It measures in length nearly six feet four inches; the greatest width at the base of the lettered surface is twelve inches, and ten towards the top of the same side; on the Ogham side it measures in depth twelve inches along its entire length. This pillar stone is one still more remarkable than that already described. It appears to be the first and, as far as is known, the only example in Ireland of a Roman and Ogham inscription co-existing and equivalents of each other on the same monument. On his first visit to Killeen Cormac, the writer perceived the Ogham scores, but the Roman letters partially escaped his observation, owing to their shallowness; besides, he was unprepared to meet with a monument of such extreme antiquity and rareness in that part of Ireland, which might be regarded as fully explored. Being, however, at Killeen Cormac on an October evening in 1860, which was showery, with intervals of bright sunshine, and then examining these monuments, the depression of the Roman letters being filled with water and glistening under the setting sun, enabled him to read distinctly the words, IVVENᴇ DʀVVIDES, and excited a most lively interest in the discovery. Rubbings were then made, and since that time very frequently and more carefully. The discovery of the Latin inscription in connection with the Ogham gave ample room for speculation. The letters IVVENE DRVVIDES, suggested the name of Dubhtach, the chief druid of king Leoghaire, whom St Patrick converted at Tara. By changing -EN- to *ach* in IVVEN-E, he began to think that the stone

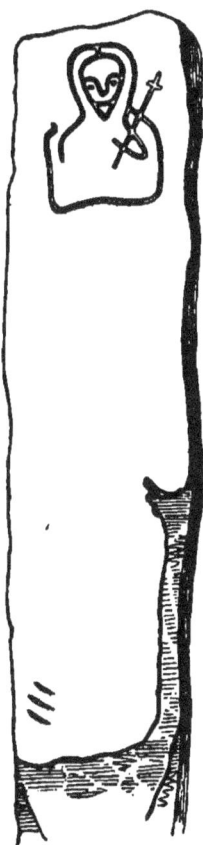

No. 2.

No. 3.ˢ

that marked the grave of Dubhtach, the druid, was lying before him. His connection with St. Fiech of Sleatty, his own territory of Hy-Kinselagh, both near at hand, his poem[1] on Enna Kinselagh, whom he styles "the hero of Magh Fine", suggested the probability of Dubhtach's remains resting in the scene of his literary labours; and where more fittingly could rest the first Christian neophyte of his order, than in one of the earliest and most honoured churches of the first Christian bishop in Ireland, his hallowed grave being marked by rude and simple monuments, on which were inscribed the distinctive characteristics of Latin and Celtic literature and civilization. These ideas received a most remarkable confirmation in an examination of the Ogham and Latin inscriptions, made by Mr. Whitley Stokes, which he communicated to the writer, after these monuments had been described in a paper read before the Royal Irish Academy (Monday, May 22, 1865), and which Mr. Stokes has since described, with two other inscriptions of a cognate character existing in Wales and Scotland, in a recent number of a German periodical.[2]

In the Killeen monuments the inscriptions are in the genitive singular governed by "lapis" understood, as is usual in Celtic monuments. The correct form of the last syllable of the in-

[1] Vide the poem ascribed to Dubhthach by Professor O'Curry, app. p. 486. In this he names "Magh fine" (Quaere—Was Magh Fine the Fin Magh or Campus Lucidus where St. Abban governed a monastery?), Mugna, and Maisden now Mullachmast, of many historic recollections in ancient as well as in modern times. Under its shadow, at Prospect House, was born, on the 29th of April, 1804, his Eminence the Cardinal Archbishop of Dublin, Quem Deus, Incol. sospit. servet.

[2] The writer of this paper begs to record the generosity of the Council of the Royal Irish Academy in lending these wood-cuts for its illustration; also his best thanks for the favour.   [3] Beiträge zür vergleichendan Sprachforschüng.

scription would be IS, rather than ES. The early Christian
monuments of the catacombs present errors of this kind. The
Ogham reads, DVFTANO SAEI SAHATTOS, which Mr.
Stokes reads thus: DVFTANO, a gen. sing. nom. Dubtanos.
In root it may be connected with Dubhtach, the last part in AN,
by a change of termination common in Irish names, becomes
OC or OG, young, little. Thus comes Dubthac, a primeval
Celtic name, a form of DVBOTANOS, meaning black, thin,
or shaggy. DVBO; Irish, ʊubh; Welsh, DU: TANOS,
Welsh, TENEN; Latin, Tenuis; Greek, ταvoς; English, *thin.*
The next word, SAEI, is a gen. sing. SAEOS, or SAIOS nom.,
equivalent to the old Irish ʄaɩ (sophos), sage, which here assu-
ming the usual loss of P, e.g. cʌuτ, for Caput, should be
equalled with the Latin sapiens. In the last word, SAHOTTOS,
the H is merely inserted to prevent the hiatus produced by
the loss of P. This word is referred to the root SAP; whence
Sapiens, Sapio, Latin; *Savoir,* French; SEFFAN, intelligere,
etc., etc. SAHOTTOS for SAPANTOS, would appear by its
form to be a gen. sing. of an adjectival stem in NT. The loss
or assimilation of N before T is to be found in old Irish partici-
pial forms, so that, in meaning as in root, SAHOTTOS may be
regarded as identical with the Latin *sapientis:* so that the Celtic
part of the inscription should be thus translated (Lapis Sepulcra-
lis) Dubtanis Sophi Sapientis, i.e. the sepulchral stone of Dubhtach the Sage of Wisdom, which nearly agrees with the terms in
which Dubhtach is described in the *Senchus Mor,* ʊubτʌċ ʄaɩ
lɩc̣ɲ. The letters of the Latin inscription are uncials or capi-
tals. A bilingual inscription on a pillar stone at St. Dog-
mael's, near Cardigan, in Wales, reads—SAGRANI FILI
CVNOTAMI. The Oghams read — SAGRAMNI MAQI
CVNATAMI. This monument is supposed to commemorate
the son of Cunedda Wledig, a Cambrian prince, A.D. 340–389.
Mr. Westwood assigns this inscription to a date not long
after the departure of the Romans from Britain. At Lann-
feckin, in Cardiganshire, and at Trelong, in Brecknock, bilingual monuments exist, having the same characteristics, though
somewhat later in point of time, as they exhibit traces of
the so-called Lombardic influence in the formation of the letters,
no traces of which exist in the Killeen inscription; so that it
differs in this respect also from the inscribed monuments of a
later period, on which the letters have a distinctive Celtic character. It may be perhaps concluded that the Killeen inscription
was incised by an artist, himself a foreigner, or at least under the
immediate instruction of one who learned to write before the
change made in the forms of the old uncials became general in
Italy. An inscription preserved in the church of St. Ursula at

Cologne,[1] exhibits letters of this class, and is referred to a period not later than the year 500 by the most learned German archaeologists. Count de Rossi, who examined them in 1860, coincided in that view, so that it may be concluded that the letters and sculpture engraved on the Killeen monuments are only the reflection of the art of the catacombs, a source from which the earliest Irish students of ecclesiastical design drew their inspirations, and founded a school which exerted a wonderful influence on the sculpture, and more vividly still on the illuminated manuscripts of western Europe, thus paying back with interest a debt of gratitude due to that country which is the common cradle of art and Christianity.   J. F. S.

UNIVERSITY EDUCATION IN IRELAND.[2]

THE prominent position you occupy in our country and among our representatives in the Imperial Parliament, and your well-known anxiety to secure for Irish Catholics an educational system in accordance with our religious principles, induce me to address the following remarks to you. They regard a question which now fills the minds of educated men in Ireland, nay, throughout the Empire. The importance of that question cannot be gainsayed, for on its right solution, perhaps more than on anything else, depends the momentous issue: Is Catholic Ireland to remain Catholic? Is the destruction of ascendancy in this country to be made the basis of religious indifferentism? or is the new era of political and social equality to be blessed by religion? Is the education of our Catholic people, which will determine the future of Ireland, and of which the university is the corner-stone, to be established, now at this turning-point of our history, on the firm and immoveable rock of Catholic truth? or is it to be laid upon a foundation whose strength and durability are doubtful? Now, as it is admitted on all hands, that our claims for educational equality are just and reasonable, the important question which I ask you to consider is: Whether a distinct Catholic University, or a Catholic University College in a common University, is likely to be the more advantageous to the religious and the educational interests of Irish Catholics? I reply without hesitation—the former; and I shall endeavour briefly to state my reasons for this opinion. However, before doing so, it may be desirable to recall to mind the actual position of the University Question.

[1] Vide *Essays on Religion and Literature*, edited by Dr. Manning, Archbishop of London, p. 255.

[2] This paper was written as a letter to the Right Hon. W. H. F. Cogan, M.P., by the Rector of the Catholic University, by whose kind permission it is here printed.

The Right Hon. the Chief Secretary for Ireland has informed the House of Commons that it is the intention of her Majesty's Government to establish a Catholic University, which, as far as circumstances would permit, should stand in the same position to Catholics as Trinity College does to Protestants. He proposes, moreover, that it should be almost independent of state control, but subject to the constant influence of public opinion, and governed in such a manner as would enable it to enter at once into competition with the older Universities.

It is not for me at present to express an opinion on the programme of her Majesty's Government; further than to say, that it seems to admit many most important principles, as, for instance, the right of Catholics to educate Catholics without let or hindrance, according to the principles of our religion; the right of our Bishops to intervene in education as guardians of faith and morals; the desirability of having education as far as possible free from state control, etc., etc.

In contradistinction to this scheme of her Majesty's Government, Mr. Fawcett, M.P. for Brighton, has given notice, that on the 29th instant, he will move in the House of Commons, that the fellowships and other honours and emoluments of Trinity College, its teaching and its government, be thrown open to all without religious distinction; in other words, that persons of any religion and of no religion should henceforth be eligible to the governing and the teaching staff of the College and University of Dublin.

The mere enunciation of Mr. Fawcett's plan appears to me sufficient to secure its rejection by every thoughtful Catholic. Only in one sense, it would seem, can any person who believes in the necessity of Catholic Education, appear in some measure to accept it; that is, in as much as it is a protest against the educational monopoly so long enjoyed by Trinity College for the good of the few, and in as much as it is a declaration that all the advantages attached by the state to University Education, ought to be common alike to all citizens. It was, I presume, chiefly for these reasons, that on a former occasion. Mr. Fawcett's motion was supported by many Catholic Members of Parliament. But, apart from these considerations and judged on its own merits exclusively, it embodies the principle of mixed Education in a marked and most objectionable form: it engrafts it upon an existing Protestant institution, which for many long years would give its present tone to the teaching and government of the place, and it proposes to settle in the metropolis of our Catholic country, and for the use of our Catholic nation, a non-Catholic College and University backed up by all the *prestige* of the antiquity, the wealth, and the learning of Trinity College.

In fact, Mr. Fawcett would not wish to disturb the present

fellows of Trinity College; he merely proposes that, as vacancies occur in the teaching and governing staff of the institution, Catholics and others should be eligible to the vacant places. But, I will ask, how long would it be before Catholics could by possibility obtain in this way the position in the College to which their numbers entitle them? How many years would elapse before they would have that preponderating influence, which, to say the least, is their right in a University pretending to represent a Catholic nation like Ireland? And when, after long years, the great majority of the chairs and other offices in the College would be occupied by Catholics, what should we have?—A mixed college! And what guarantee should we have for the permanency of this preponderating power of Catholics in the College? And even if it were permanent, what security should we have for the safety of the faith and morals of Catholic youth? Where is there any mention of the authority of the bishops—the divinely appointed guardians of the Christian flock?

I may be told that such an institution would be preferable to the University and its College in their present form. I answer: far from being so, it would be much more objectionable. For it is better that Catholics, when they enter a non-Catholic University, should know the dangers to which they expose themselves, than that, allured by a false semblance of liberality, they should imagine themselves safe where the perils are greatest, because in part hidden. Better to face an avowed opponent, than to rely upon a false friend. At present Catholics entering Trinity College know the dangers that threaten them. In Mr. Fawcett's plan these dangers would be concealed under the specious cloak of liberality. Again: so long as our Protestant fellow-countrymen require university education, it is far better they should have it in an institution where religion is honoured, at least externally, than that they should be compelled to seek it in halls from which even her sacred name is banished, and which eschew all her hallowing influences. The chapel of Trinity College, although not sanctified by the Sacramental presence of Him from whom ought to proceed the strength and holiness of truth in a seat of learning, is still the representative of a holy idea: it announces to the Protestant youth who crosses the threshold of that University, that learning to be fruitful of good must be based upon religion, must cluster round it, must not grovel upon earth, but must look up to heaven.

Of course, we do not desire that the advantages enjoyed by Trinity College should be monopolised by any one religious body. As far as the endowments of the University of Dublin and of Trinity College have been given by Parliament or the Crown, they were intended for the benefit not of a fraction of our people, but of the nation, and ought to be made available for that purpose.

Again, Trinity College being a Protestant institution, we have no wish to see its advantages confined to one denomination of Protestants. But this is, after all, a matter to be settled by the Protestants of Ireland among themselves, or by the wisdom of Parliament. When the Anglican Church ceases to be established by law in Ireland, there seems no reason why that body should have a preponderating position among other Protestants in the Protestant University, unless, indeed, Trinity College be looked upon as occupying for them the place which Maynooth College fills for Catholics. However, in the settlement of such a question, Parliament would, without doubt, bear in mind that, with the exception of the Presbyterians, who are but a very small fraction of the population in Leinster, Munster, and Connaught,[1] and are well provided for in Belfast, the Episcopalians, or members of the Church of England, are the only numerous body of Protestants in this country; that, in fact, all the other Protestants together do not amount to more than a few thousands, viz.: to less than three per cent. of the whole population. Parliament ought to find no practical difficulty in dealing satisfactorily with this small minority, and in fully protecting their constitutional rights.

I shall, therefore, dismiss Mr. Fawcett's scheme, as utterly wanting in the conditions requisite for obtaining the support of Irish Catholics, and as being such—to use the excellent remark of Mr. Monsell in the House of Commons last year— as would deprive Trinity College of the confidence of Protestants, and not gain for it the confidence of Catholics.

However, as the learned Member for Brighton, and others who agree with him, have proved that they mean kindly to Ireland by supporting measures most useful to our country; and as they advocate those measures because they are demanded by the great bulk of our people; let us hope that, laying aside for once their own peculiar views respecting education, those distinguished men will for the same reason give a new and most convincing proof of the sincerity of their good wishes for Ireland, by aiding the effort to establish the University system which is in accordance with the wishes and demands of the great majority of the Irish people.

I now come to the special subject of this letter. Permit me, then, briefly to consider the relative merits of the two schemes; the advantages and disadvantages of a Catholic University College in a common university on the one hand, and on the other hand, of a distinct Catholic University.

[1] According to the census of 1861, the Presbyterians are not 1 in 100 of the population in the three provinces just named; in Leinster they are ·7 per cent., or seven in every thousand persons; and in Munster and Connaught ·3, or only three in every thousand.

The advantages of a Catholic College in a National University may be summed up in one sentence: it would afford us the widest range of competition, and give us at the same time separate education for Catholics.

I. The great, indeed the paramount, advantage of competition is admitted upon all hands. By it emulation is kept up among youth, their latent energies are evoked, and their intellectual powers developed to the utmost. A system then, which brings into competition all the youth of the nation, must possess great educational advantages above any other, and such, precisely, is a National University, where all the intellect of the country would have to compete in a common arena for degrees, honours, and other literary and scientific distinctions. Moreover, this emulation would be increased by the fact, that there would be among the various colleges, a struggle for intellectual superiority, which could not fail to be productive of the greatest advantages to literature and science, each striving to out-do the others in the race, in which all would be entered.

II. Again, the students of the Catholic College having won, as no doubt they would win, distinctions in the intellectual arena, not only would their equality or superiority with respect to their Protestant fellow-countrymen be admitted at once, and this without any of that hesitation or delay, which is sure to occur before their literary or scientific standing will be recognized, if their passport to distinction bear the signature of an exclusive institution; but also the great question, whether in truth Catholic education does cramp the human mind, would be decided by a tribunal whose authority Protestants and Catholics must admit alike. In a mixed community, such as exists in these countries, it is of the greatest moment, that the university stamp should not be one which would almost ostracize the bearer, and cut him off from his fellow-countrymen, either by his own act or by their unwillingness to admit the value of the coinage; the literary and scientific coin should be such as would run current throughout the realm, because its value would be known to all. In other words, it is most important for the social interests of Catholics, that the university degree borne by them should be a *bona fide* mark of distinction, won in open competition with their fellow-countrymen of all denominations; and not the result of a hole-and-corner examination, and the fruit of work done under the inspection of a few Catholic teachers, approved and rewarded by them, and of the value of which others would know little or nothing. It is also of the greatest importance that the true intellectual value of Catholic education should be publicly proved and recognized by all.

The two most important advantages, then, of the plan which

would give us a college in the National University are: the great increase in the area of competition, and the enlarged value of the degrees and honours. And these advantages would be obtained without infringement of the principle of Catholic Education; in as much as there would be no interference with the constitution or teaching of the College, to which the whole work of educating Catholics would be entrusted. The advocates of this plan, therefore, conclude, that by it the Catholics of Ireland would have secured for them, first, the best education possible, because of the great competition; secondly, the highest rewards, because of the universal recognition of the value of the education imparted by the Catholic college, and of the degrees granted by the National University; and thirdly, complete security for the faith and morals of Catholic youth, because of the constitution and teaching of the Catholic University College.

But while admitting that these reasons are weighty, permit me to say, that they seem far from convincing; and especially of we compare them with the arguments which prove the advantage, if not the necessity, on Catholic grounds, of a distinct University for the Catholics of Ireland.

And first, as to the competition offered by a common national university, it would, of course, be a great advantage; but is it indispensable as a condition for successfully educating our Catholic people? Where does such competition exist at present in the University of Dublin? And still that institution gets on, and has got on for three hundred years very well without it. The students of Trinity College have to compete; but it is where the students of the Catholic University also would be obliged to win their way, viz., in the battle of life, in the public service, etc.

Again: would it be fair to ask the Catholic College to compete in its young and incomplete state with an old and wealthy institution like Trinity College, and especially on ground, in the selection of which the Protestant College would for years to come have a vastly preponderating influence?

The competition between a Catholic College and a Protestant one would be most useful; but is it indispensable? and might not too dear a price be paid for the advantages it would offer? Might not these advantages be purchased by the loss of still greater ones? The competition which it is sought to secure would be between the contingent furnished by the Catholic millions and that which 650,000 Protestants would supply. Would we not have enough of our own for a most healthy competition? And especially if a number of distinct colleges were to arise in our Catholic University, as they would be sure to arise in a very short time.

Would the injury inflicted by the absence of the non-Catholic contingent be really so great?

Let our schools and colleges, banded together under their own Catholic University, only get fair play; let the development of colleges in the University itself only be allowed to proceed without let or hindrance; let high intellectual culture in science and literature be fostered among Catholics, and in accordance with the principles of our religion, as has been done for Protestants on the principles of Protestantism for the last three hundred years; and we shall soon make the greatest enemies of Catholicity admit that her teaching does not cramp the intellect or enslave the mind, and that Irish Catholics are nowise inferior to their fellow-countrymen of other denominations.

But this train of argument has led us naturally to the more intrinsic, and the fundamental objection to this plan of a common university.

The government of a common university would be vested in a council or senate, either made up of representatives of the various university colleges, or, as is the case in the Queen's University, appointed entirely or in great part by the Crown. In either plan, where would be the safeguard for the faith and morals of Catholic youth? Is it in the teaching and discipline of the Catholic college? This would be far from sufficient. If the University mean anything, indeed if competition among its students is to be possible, it must have the power not only of electing examiners, but also of prescribing courses of studies, of enjoining or recommending class-books and books of reference, etc. Now, are we willing to leave the settlement of these most important questions to a council, where Catholics will be in the minority, or at any rate, where there will be no one to speak authoritatively as to the requirements for the due preservation of the faith and morals of Catholics?

I shall be told, that the university council would not mix itself up with these matters of detail; that it would confine itself to the appointment of subjects, leaving to the colleges the choice of books. Whatever we may think of this answer in theory, the practice has been quite different; witness the arrangements proposed under the Supplemental Charter of the Queen's University, which I shall have occasion later to consider more fully; witness the London University, where, I understand, the gravest questions have from time to time arisen with the Catholic colleges respecting the books to be used, the curriculum of studies, etc.

And is it to be supposed that the tendencies of a university and of its examiners will not be known to the students, and will not have the greatest influence upon the formation of their principles? Any one who thinks that they will not, shows how utterly unacquainted he is with human nature and with the circumstances which exert the greatest influence on the pliant mind of youth. The words, the looks, the very thoughts of teachers and examiners, are scanned and copied, often unconsciously.

Again, what will be the subjects in which the wished for competition is to be created and fostered? History, mental philosophy, ethics, political economy; many others, in which it is of the last importance that true principles should be instilled into the minds of youth. And how can these principles be put forward and cherished under a mixed council, and under an authority which has no religious principle of its own? by a body which deals with these important issues merely as expediency suggests? Will we omit these subjects in a National University, or will we suffer the minds of our Catholic youth to be moulded by an institution which has no fixed principles, and whose office it must be to neutralize, as far as possible, the Catholic tendencies which it is the duty of a Catholic college to impart to its alumni?

The capital objection, then, to this plan of a common university is, that although the office of teaching Catholics in the Catholic college would be entrusted to Catholics, still that most important duty would be discharged under the direction of the common university, which would have the right not alone of examining the students, to which we could not object, but also of fixing beforehand the curriculum and all other particulars regarding the studies; in other words, a mixed senate would be put at the head of the education of our Catholic country. Who is there, that does not see, that thus would be realized in a great measure the description given by the Sacred Congregation of the dangers inherent in the frequentation by Catholics of a non-Catholic university?

"In the present case, where, as his Holiness has declared, those who frequent the (non-Catholic) universities incur an intrinsic and grievous danger to purity of morals, as well as to faith (which is absolutely necessary to salvation), who can fail to see that it is next to impossible to discover circumstances which would allow Catholics, without sin, to attend non-Catholic universities? The light and unstable minds of youth; the errors which in such institutions are imbibed, almost through the atmosphere, without being counteracted by more solid doctrine; the very great power which human respect and the taunts of companions exercise upon young men, lead them so rapidly and so immediately into the danger of falling, that generally no sufficient reason can be conceived why young men should be entrusted to these universities".—*Letter from the Propaganda to the English Bishops.*

The dangers thus graphically described would be found in a great measure in the common university; and the supreme control of the education of the country would be given to a mixed board, that is to a senate or university, which in its corporate capacity would have no religion, and could have none.

But the greatest evils might also arise from the professors to whom the duty of teaching would be entrusted in a mixed university. It is true, the teachers in the Catholic University College might be everything we could desire. But it must not be forgotten, that, besides the college teachers, there would also be a certain number of university professors. These would be appointed by the council of the university, or in some other way to be fixed by the charter. But in their appointment there would be no guarantee whatsoever for the soundness of their principles. It is true, attendance on their lectures would not be obligatory; but still every student of the University would have a right to attend them, whatever the college to which he belonged. These university professors would be the great luminaries of the university; the frequentation of their lectures would be of immense advantage to such students as might wish to make a special study of the particular subject; and the influence wielded by such men in a learned university would be incredible. Thus, for instance, in Oxford, Dr. Pusey is specially attached to Christ Church; but he is also University Professor of Hebrew; his lectures are available for the students of all the colleges; his influence is felt throughout the whole university. Now in the case of an Irish National University, many of the university professorships might be held by men whose teaching would be heterodox, and whose opinions would be rationalistic; it would be impossible to prevent our Catholic youth from frequenting their teaching; and, as they would be men of admitted ability and often of most fascinating manners, many might be drawn into the vortex of their errors, and carried into the abyss of indifferentism or infidelity. For instance, take history, that most important branch of human knowledge: the professor selected by a mixed board to represent that department in the National University of Ireland, despite the incongruity of the appointment in this thoroughly religious land, might be a M. Renan, or the author of the *History of Rationalism*. It is true, the learned Professor Robertson would continue to teach the sound principles of historical science to the Catholic students; but who can tell the corrupting effects of the erroneous teaching which would be supposed to represent the university? And who would not tremble for the future of our country, when he remembered the words of Divine Wisdom: *Fascinatio enim nugacitatis obscurat bona, et inconstantia concupiscentiae transvertit sensum sine malitia,*

("The bewitching of folly obscureth good things, and the inconstancy of concupiscence overturneth the innocent mind".)

But I may be told, that the senate or council of the University need not be made up exclusively of the representatives of the Catholic and Protestant colleges, but might be a body appointed by the crown, or by some other external authority, as is done in the senate of the Queen's University, and that in such a body the religious interests of Catholics would be protected. Waiving the point as to whether the safeguards would then be sufficient in the judgment of those, who alone are our guides in such matters, I find that another most serious difficulty meets us. I mean the great defect of not having within the university itself a supreme educational authority, to which the students would look for the *corona* of their academical course. When I visited the University of Louvain in 1861, I understood from the illustrious Rector-Magnificus, the late Monsignor de Ram, that he and his learned associates found the system of sending their students to an *external* tribunal for degrees very unsatisfactory; and he impressed on me the great advantage of having degrees which would emanate from the University itself, that is, from the body which taught, and governed, and moulded the minds of the academical youth. The educational evils arising from the opposite system are well explained in the following official paper quoted by Major O'Reilly, in his able pamphlet on University Education. The extract is taken from the *Rapport sur l' enseignement supérieur en Prusse, présenté en Mars 1845, a M. Nothomb, Ministre de l'Interieur, par Charles Looman. Brussels*, 1860.

"The Belgian Universities do all that they can; but sooner or later they will feel the evil effects of the law on superior instruction. Science, instead of enjoying a little freedom, and producing large and varied developments, is ill at ease under the yoke of the programmes of examinations. Professors, situated as they are, cannot fail to lose some of their devotion to science. The majority of the students have not a scientific spirit; their studies are generally confined to a knowledge of abridgments and a superficial gloss of learning, which the Germans familiarly call *brod-studium*. The subjects for examination are too numerous; it is a general defect of the law of 1835 to favour what may be called *polymathy*. It is a commonsense truth, that it is better to study well one subject than to acquire a smattering of many. I might extend these observations to all the branches of study. Why do the regulations concerning examinations force the professors to follow over the same track? By increasing beyond measure the subjects of examination, the law obliges the examiners to come to a tacit agreement amongst themselves as to the course of examination. Thus it is understood nowa-days that the examination on the history of philosophy shall comprise only ancient philosophy; that on Greek shall consist in being able to translate one or two books of Homer. This is what our system of examinations has brought us to".

From this admirable statement I conclude, that it is of the greatest importance for education that the programme of examinations, etc., should not be fixed by an authority external to the teaching bodies; otherwise the education will not have that pliability which is desirable, but will run as it were in a groove, and the intellectual development of the nation will be nipped in the bud and stunted.

But I may be told, that these inconveniences are more than counterbalanced by the great advantage of unity of education, and, consequently, unity of national feeling, which would be the fruit of one common university, and could never proceed from various denominational universities. My answer is very plain: an argument which proves too much, proves nothing. If this reasoning have any weight, it would prove the advantage or necessity of mixed education in order to consolidate the nation. Now both reason and experience show, that this effect does not follow from mixed education; some who were most strenuous in supporting the mixed system, in order to unite the people, begin now at last to see that the union of men's hearts is not to be attained by banishing religion from the school, but by impressing more and more upon the minds of youth the golden precepts of Christian charity, which is founded on faith.

But is it not notorious that the multiplication of universities will bring decadence in study and in learning, and a desire to undersell each other?

I do not think this consequence is, by any means, necessary: it does not follow in Germany; it has not followed in Ireland since the foundation of the Queen's University, nor in England since the establishment of the University of London. And if such a danger be apprehended, it would not be difficult to secure the universities against it by some prudent enactments, and by removing the temptation for the sale of degrees. But have not we the same reason, or an equal one, for supposing that the multiplication of universities, instead of weakening learning, would only increase the competition among the students, and raise the tone of all the colleges, and of the universities themselves? The experience of life in other matters would make us think so. Competition, if it often lead to adulteration and underselling, is generally, on the whole, beneficial to the public, and brings into the market better articles and in greater variety.

Before concluding this part of my subject, permit me to add, that the experience of the Supplemental Charter of 1866, and of the programme drawn up under it, convinced me of the extreme difficulty, not to say the impossibility, of a mixed senate's devising arrangements which would be in every way satisfactory to Catholics, and under which the Catholic college would continue to work for any considerable length of time. In the programme to which I refer, the mental and moral sciences were far from occupying the position they ought to hold in the educational system by which a Catholic nation, like Ireland, is to be trained; and books were appointed, or at least suggested, which are not the most desirable for our Catholic youth, while the great standard authors of Catholic Europe were omitted or scarcely noticed. Now, that programme, most certainly, was framed with the view of meeting Catholic views as far as possible; and if such grave inconveniences can be detected in it, they or still greater would surely be found in the working out of the common university.

In conclusion, permit me to say that I see no objection to common examiners for Catholics and Protestants, provided they have no control, direct or indirect, over the course of studies, or over their students or their teachers. Indeed there seems a certain weight in the objection raised against Trinity College, viz.: that there the same persons teach, examine, and give degrees. And the great man and learned scholar who first filled the rectorial chair in our Catholic University seems to have adopted a much more effectual course for the protection of the intellectual interests of his pupils, when he ordered that no person should examine in a faculty in which he was a professor.

I shall now briefly consider the advantages to be found in a distinct Catholic University.

And, in the first place, I set down the advantages implied in the very idea of a university; advantages which cannot be realized for Catholics, unless the university be under the aegis of the Church; unless its animating principle be religion; that is, unless it be a distinct Catholic University. For what is a university? I cannot answer better than in the eloquent words of Dr. Newman:—

"A university is a place of concourse, whither students come from every quarter for every kind of knowledge. You cannot have the best of every kind everywhere; you must go to some great city or emporium for it. There you have all the choicest productions of nature and art altogether, which you find each in its separate place elsewhere. All the riches of the land, and of the world, are carried up thither; there are the best markets, and there the best workmen. It is the centre of trade, the supreme court of fashion, the umpire of rival skill, and the standard of things rare and precious. It is the

444   University Education in Ireland.

place for seeing galleries of first-rate pictures, and for hearing wonderful voices and miraculous performers. It is the place for great preachers, great orators, great nobles, great statesmen. In the nature of things, greatness and unity go together; excellence implies a centre. Such, then, for the third or fourth time, is a University; I hope I do not weary out the reader by repeating it. It is the place to which a thousand schools make contributions; in which the intellect may safely range and speculate, sure to find its equal in some antagonist activity, and its judge in the tribunal of truth. It is a place where inquiry is pushed forward, and discoveries verified and perfected, and rashness rendered innocuous, and error exposed, by the collision of mind with mind, and knowledge with knowledge. It is the place where the professor becomes eloquent, and a missionary and preacher of science, displaying it in its most complete and most winning form, pouring it forth with the zeal of enthusiasm, and lighting up his own love in the breasts of hearers. It is the place where the catechist makes good his ground as he goes, treading in the truth day by day into the ready memory, and wedging and tightening it into the expanding reason. It is a place which attracts the affections of the young by its fame, wins the judgment of the middle-aged by its beauty, and rivets the memory of the old by its associations. It is a seat of wisdom, a light of the world, a minister of the faith, an Alma Mater of the rising generation. It is this and a great deal more, and demands a somewhat better head and hand than mine to describe it well.

"Such it is in its idea and in its purpose; such in good measure has it before now been in fact. Shall it ever be again? We are going forward in the strength of the Cross, under the patronage of Mary, in the name of Patrick, to attempt it".

Could a mere college in a common university realize all this? I am convinced it could not.

Secondly, it is most desirable that the mind of a nation like ours should not be forced into one mould; that a certain liberty should be allowed, in order to produce various kinds of mental culture; in a special manner it is to be wished for that the Catholic intelligence of our nation should be evoked and developed to the full; that it should be brought into contact with the Catholic intellect of the continent, with their books, their mode of teaching, their thoughts, their feelings, their habits; that, on the one hand, Ireland's forced isolation from Europe, which has existed for so many centuries, should cease; and on the other hand, that a new phase of mental culture should be produced, which would be at once adapted to the wants of the age, Irish, and Catholic. All this could not be done in a mere college of a mixed university; it could only be done in a truly Catholic University.

Finally, the work given to our race to accomplish could

never be achieved by a mere college, or by a university made up of heterogeneous elements. The eloquent words of Newman explain this argument far better than I can pretend to do, and with them I conclude:—

"I see an age of transition, the breaking up of the old and the coming in of the new; an old system shattered some sixty years ago, and a new state of things scarcely in its rudiments yet, to be settled perhaps some centuries after our time. And it is a special circumstance in these changes, that they extend beyond the historical platform of human affairs; not only is Europe broken up, but other continents are thrown open, and the new organization of society aims at embracing the world. It is a day of colonists and emigrants;—and, what is another most pertinent consideration, the language they carry with them is English, which consequently, as time goes on, is certain, humanly speaking, to extend itself into every part of the world. It is already occupying the whole of North America, whence it threatens to descend upon the South; already it has become the speech of a hundred marts of commerce, scattered over the East, and, even where not the mother tongue, it is at least the medium of intercourse between nations. And lastly, though the people who own that language is Protestant, a race preëminently Catholic has adopted it, and has a share in its literature; and this Catholic race is, at this very time, of all tribes of the earth, the most fertile in emigrants both to the West and the South. These are the facts of the day, which we should see before our eyes, whether the Pope had anything to say to them or no. The English language and the Irish race are overrunning the world.

"When then I consider what an eye the Sovereign Pontiffs have for the future; and what an independence in policy and vigour in action have been the characteristics of their present representative; and what a flood of success, mounting higher and higher, has lifted up the Ark of God from the beginning of this century; and then, that the Holy Father has definitely put his finger upon Ireland, and selected her soil as the seat of a great Catholic University, to spread religion, science, and learning, wherever the English language is spoken; when I take all these things together,—I care not what others do, God has no need of men,—oppose who will, shrink who will, I know and cannot doubt that a great work is begun. It is no great imprudence to commit oneself to a guidance which never yet has failed; nor is it surely irrational or fanatical to believe, that, whatever difficulties or disappointments, reverses or delays, may be our lot in the prosecution of the work, its ultimate success is certain, even though it seems at first to fail,—just as the greatest measures in former times have been the longest in carrying out, as Athanasius triumphed though he passed away before Arianism, and Hildebrand died in exile, that his successors might enter into his labours".

I resume. In a common university with a Catholic college we have the following advantages:—

Firstly, The greatest extent of competition, and consequent increase of emulation among the students.

Secondly, The increased value of distinctions and degrees.

Thirdly, Catholic teaching for Catholic youth.

On the other hand, it would seem that four and a half millions of Irish Catholics, besides the millions of English-speaking Catholics throughout the world, ought to be able to furnish ample materials for competition without recurring to a common university; more especially since in it there would be no sufficient safeguard for the faith and morals of Catholics against any inimical influence on the part of the university. That this influence would be great is clear, because to the university would belong the right not only of electing examiners, but also of appointing courses of studies, subjects for examinations, conditions for obtaining honours, etc. The dangers to be guarded against are also seen from the subjects, to which the university examinations must extend; history, mental philosophy, etc.

Finally; the influence for good or evil to be exercised by the university professors, as distinguished from the professors in the Catholic college, shows how unsafe the faith and morals of Catholics would be in a mixed university, even although we should have a Catholic college.

On the other hand, there would be great educational defects, if the senate or council of the university were quite external to the colleges.

All these reasons against the attempt to unite a Catholic college with others under a mixed university, are confirmed by the experience of the Supplemental Charter of 1866, and of the difficulties which Catholic colleges find in working with the London University.

On the other hand, the advantages of a distinct Catholic university are, precisely, those which caused the work to be set on foot originally.

First, the fulness of Catholic teaching, under the aegis of the Church.

Secondly, the variety of mental culture, by breaking down the wall of separation, which separates us from the continent, bringing us into contact with the Catholic intellect of Europe.

Thirdly, the mission given to Catholic Ireland, to work out among the English-speaking inhabitants of the globe.

I conclude by recalling the noble vision conjured up by the great man, on whom I have already drawn so largely; and I ask first, can that bright vision ever be realized if we place at the head of our education a mixed university; and secondly, are we prepared to forego our chance of such a glorious future?

"Looking at the general state of things at this day, I desiderate for a school of the Church, if an additional school is to be granted to us, a more central position than Oxford has to show. Since the age of Alfred and of the first Henry, the world has grown, from the west and south of Europe, into four or five continents; and I look for a city less inland than that old sanctuary, and a country closer upon the highway of the seas. I look towards a land both old and young; old in its Christianity, young in the promise of its future: a nation, which received grace before the Saxon came to Britain, and which has never quenched it; a Church, which comprehends in its history the rise and fall of Canterbury and York, which Augustine and Paulinus found, and Pole and Fisher left behind them. I contemplate a people which has had a long night, and will have an inevitable day. I am turning my eyes towards a hundred years to come, and I dimly see the island I am gazing on, become the road of passage and union between two hemispheres, and the centre of the world. I see its inhabitants rival Belgium in populousness, France in vigour, and Spain in enthusiasm; and I see England taught by advancing years to exercise in its behalf that good sense which is her characteristic towards every one else. The capital of that prosperous and hopeful land is situate in a beautiful bay and near a romantic region; and in it I see a flourishing University, which for a while had to struggle with fortune, but when its first founders and servants were dead and gone, had successes far exceeding their anxieties. Thither, as to a sacred soil, the home of their fathers, and the fountain-head of their Christianity, students are flocking from East, West, and South, from America and Australia and India, from Egypt and Asia Minor, with the ease and rapidity of a locomotion not yet discovered, and last, though not least, from England,— all speaking one tongue, all owning one faith, all eager for one large true wisdom, and thence, when their stay is over, going back again to carry peace to men of good will over all the earth".

I have the honour to remain, dear sir,
Your faithful servant,
BARTH. WOODLOCK, Rector.

CATHOLIC UNIVERSITY,
Dublin, 8th May, 1868.

P.S.—Since writing these lines, I have been favoured with the following letter from the Rector Magnificus of the University of Louvain, the Right Rev. Monsignor Laforet. I append it, as it may be interesting to you and others to know the views of a man so distinguished for his learning and experience:—

Université Catholique de Louvain,
Louvain, le 6 Mai, 1868.

MONSEIGNEUR,

En réponse à votre lettre du premier de ce mois, je m' empresse de vous dire, que vous devez, à mon avis, maintenir l' indépen-

dance complète de votre Université, et que vous ne pouvez pas permet-
tre que vos élèves subissent des examens devant un jury mixte, composé
de professeurs Protestants et Catholiques.   Je verrais dans ce régime
de très grands inconvenients, dès aujourd'hui, pour vos leçons et
pour les études des jeunes gens Catholiques, et je redouterais des
dangers plus grands pour l'avenir.   Comment enseigner l'histoire
surtout et le droit public si vos élèves doivent répondre à des juges
Protestants ?   Que de faux tempéraments, que de regrettables accom-
modements ne seraient pas à craindre !   Tout votre système d'enseignement superieur en souffrirait nécessairement.   Puis, que de
difficultés dans la composition des jurys, que de tiraillements dans
le sein des juges !   N'allez pas sacrifier votre indépendence, le plus
précieux des biens et au point de vue moral et même au point de vue
scientifique, à un vain espoir d'une plus grande émulation pour vos
élèves.   Il y a un moyen très simple d' exciter l' émulation des jeunes
gens et au même temps de donner de la valeur aux grades académiques, c'est de se montrer sévère dans la collation de ces grades,
comme nous le faisons ici dans la faculté de théologie, où nous
sommes tout à fait libres.

Il serait risquer de tout perdre que d'admettre une seule université en Irlande, composée de deux colléges, l'une Catholique,
l'autre Protestant !

Il est vrai, le système des jurys mixtes ou combinés n'offre pas en
Belgique de très grands inconveniants.   Mais nôtre situation n'est
pas la même que la vôtre.   D'abord, l'université de Louvain ne
siège jamais qu' avec l'une ou l'autre des deux universités de l'Etat
(Liège et Gand) dont tous les professeurs sont Catholiques, au moins
de nom, et respectent les croyances de nos élèves dans leurs inter-
rogations ; ensuite, nos élèves sont *principalement* interrogés par leurs
propres professeurs, les autres interrogent peu ; enfin plusieurs des
cours académiques ne sont pas l'objet de cet examen par le jury.
Malgré tous ces tempéraments, notre système offre encore des inconvenients.   Gardez-vous donc de nous imiter sous ce rapport en
Irlande.   Un tel système dans un pays où les juges Cátholiques
seraient melés aux juges Protestants, serait désastreux.   Tâchez
d'obtenir pour cette chère université Catholique à laquelle nous
portons un si vif intérêt, une charte qui lui permette de s'adminis-
trer et de se gouverner en toutes choses sans aucune intervention
étrangère.

Je serais toujours heureux de vous fournir tous les renseignements
dont vous pourriez avoir besoin.

Agréez, Monseigneur et vénéré confrère, l' hommage de mes sen-
timents bien devoués en N. S. J. C.

N. J. LAFORET, *Rect. Univ.*

A Monseigneur Barth. Woodlock,
    Recteur de l' Université Cath. d' Irlande.

SUBTERRANEAN ROME.

1. *Introduction.*—The impulse given of late years to the study of sacred archaeology is certainly not the least among the glories of the splendid pontificate of Pius the Ninth. To his munificence, mainly, do we owe it that the monuments of the early Christians, so long shrouded in the gloom of the Roman catacombs, have been placed before the world in the fullest light of accurate scientific research. It is true that the catacombs have not been described now for the first time. As far back as 1593, Antonio Bosio, who has been happily styled the Columbus of subterranean Rome, had already commenced those visits to the underground Christian cemeteries, which were to occupy him for thirty-six laborious years. And from his day down to our own, there never have been wanting patient explorers and zealous topograpers of the hidden treasure-houses of the early Christians. But, much as we reverence these men—and it is not easy to tell how much they deserve our reverence—we must acknowledge that the result of their labours still left much to be desired. We rarely find in any of these writers that happy union of erudition with good sense, of precise statement with critical acumen, which are qualities essentially requisite for the perfect accomplishment of the task they had proposed to themselves to achieve. Hence, the science they loved so much came to be looked on as eminently unsatisfactory, and wanting in that precision and solidity which alone can command attention and respect. It was reserved for the Cavalier de Rossi above all others to import into archaeological controversies the elements in which they were hitherto too frequently deficient, and to reconstruct on a new and surer basis the entire science of Christian antiquities. In this undertaking he was encouraged by Pius the Ninth, who not only favoured him with his patronage, but contributed out of his scanty resources the means wherewith he might continue the work of the excavations, and set before the public the results therefrom derived. The first volume of de Rossi's work, published by order of Pius the Ninth, appeared in 1864; the second has just been given to the public.[1] The subject matter of these volumes is one of surpassing interest. It is, in very truth, a history of the beginning of Christianity. It examines the monuments of our earliest fathers in the faith which time has spared, and from each marble and coloured glass and fresco and sepulchral slab collects

[1] *La Roma Sotterranea Cristiana, descritta ed illustrata dal Cav. G. B. de Rossi,* publicata per ordine della Santità di N. S. Papa Pio Nono. Tomo i, con

testimony to show what manner of belief and of worship was dear to those whose faith and practice were moulded after the model of the apostles and by the labour of the apostles themselves. Our readers will find in the sketch we proceed to lay before them, that many and many a difficulty, urged by modern rationalism and heresy against the Catholic Church, is completely solved by those dispassionate witnesses, speaking after the lapse of so many ages, from the consecrated resting places of the martyrs.

2. *Authors who have written about the Catacombs.*—It will be useful to premise, by way of introduction, a short account of the authors who have hitherto treated of subterranean Rome. Ciacconius, de Winghe, John l'Heureux, better known by his Greek name of Macarius, explored the catacombs discovered in 1578. But, as we have mentioned above, it was Antonio Bosio who first founded the study of Christian archaeology. During thirty-six years he made sketches of every object of interest he was enabled to discover in his underground journeys. He died in 1629, before he could publish his book. It was only in 1632–1635 that Father Severano, of the Oratory, edited, with some additions of his own, the result of Bosio's learned labours.[1] In 1651, another Oratorian, Father Aringhi, published a Latin translation of Bosio's book,[2] making some additions of his own which were of little or no value. The plan adopted by Bosio of registering on the spot the discoveries of each day, unfortunately now fell into disuse. The sacred antiquities were no longer explained by men who in person directed the excavations, but by scholars, who in the retirement of their cabinets composed ingenious dissertations on the materials collected by their predecessors. Thus Fabretti[3] described the inscriptions of two cemeteries lately discovered. Boldetti[4] published the result of more than thirty years' excava-

atlante di xl. tavole, Roma, 1864, pp. 351, app. 85; tom. ii., con atlante di lxvii. tavole, pp. 391; app. 134. Roma, 1868. The dedication is contained in the following elegant inscription:—

Pio. IX. Pont. Max.
Alteri. Damaso.
Qui. Monumenta. Martyrum. Xti.
Miliarii. Seculi. Ruinis. Obruta
In. Lucem. Revocat
Haec. Volumina. Jussu. Ejus. Confecta
Auctor.
D. D.

[1] *Roma Sotterranea*, Rome, 1632–1635, *folio.*
[2] *Roma Subterranea novissima post Antonium Bosium et Joannem Severanum*, 2 vols. fol., Roma, 1651-1659.
[3] *Inscriptionum antiquarum explicatio.* Roma, 1699, in folio.
[4] *Osservazioni sopra i cimiteri de' santi martiri ed antichi Christiani di' Roma.* Roma, folio, 1720.

tions, but his work is disfigured by great carelessness. Marangoni[1] and Lupi also contributed much to sacred science. Bottari,[2] who came next, and ranked high as an authority, preferred the work of Boldetti to that of Bosio, and is deficient in knowledge of the local peculiarities of the catacombs. He was the last of those who devoted themselves to the exploration of the subterranean cemeteries, until in our own time another race of archaeologists arose. But in the interval, owing to the prevailing neglect of original research, the erroneous opinions advanced by Burnet and other Protestants were adopted even by some Catholics. In modern times, Settele, Rostell, Raoul-Rochette, and above all, Father Marchi, who commenced in 1841, inaugurated a new and better school. Among those who assisted Father Marchi in preparing his work on the architecture of Christian subterranean Rome, was Cavalier J. B. de Rossi, whose latest work has suggested the present paper.

3. *Situation and extent of the Catacombs.*—The ancient Christian cemeteries at Rome, commonly called the catacombs, occupy a zone of from about one to two miles in width around the walls of the city. Their extent is surprising. The superficies which they occupy is not indeed excessively large, but what mainly constitutes their vast extent is the number of their passages, or corridors, which are excavated in different levels, there being sometimes as many as four or five stories, one over the other. An exact measurement has shown that in a space of one hundred and twenty-five feet square there is not less than half a mile of passages; and the total sum of all the lines of excavation seems to reach the prodigious figure of about three hundred and sixty miles, almost the entire length of Italy. Formerly it was believed by many even among the learned, and the opinion still lingers in the popular traditions, that the various threads of this immense underground net-work were all connected one with the other, and that the communication between their parts was uninterrupted. But the Tiber, which intervenes, and the geological condition of the land, forbid such a theory. It would be simply impossible to open a communication between the necropolis on the northern and that on the southern side of the river. And this conclusion, suggested by science, is fully borne out by history and experience. We learn from authentic sources, that in the third century the Roman Church had twenty-six distinct cemeteries, which number corresponds precisely to the number of

---

[1] *Acta S. Victorini*, Roma, 4to, 1640; *Dissertatio ad . . . . Severae martyri epitaphium.* Panormi, 1784.

[2] *Sculture e pitture sagre estratte dai cimiteri di Roma.* Roma, 3 vols. in folio, 1734–1754.

the parishes then in existence within the city. Some other isolated excavations, or subterranean monuments, belonging to martyrs or to some Christian families, add to this number twenty more, so that we have in all about forty-six catacombs, or cemeteries, in close neighbourhood one to the other, and containing in their galleries several millions of tombs.

4. *Causes that led to their formation.*—These cemeteries owe their formation to the Catholic doctrine of the resurrection of the body. Many reasons combined to recommend to the early Christians the practice, then general, of burning the bodies of the dead. Such a plan would not require great space; it would better enable them to conceal their numbers; and in times of persecution would lessen the dangers that surrounded them. But their faith in the resurrection, and the respect naturally felt by a Christian for that flesh which has been sanctified by so many sacraments, and especially by One, taught them to forego all these advantages, and to expend their tenderest care in honouring the lifeless clay which was one day to appear once more before God. Hence they used to wash it, to anoint it with sweet spices in imitation of what was done at our Lord's burial, and even to embalm it. Nor would they fling into a common trench the remains of their departed brethren, as the pagans were wont to do with the corpses of the poor and of the slaves; each body should have its own proper place of rest, and as near as possible to the last remains of a martyr. Hence arose the wide-extending cemeteries, or *places of rest*, which name is the special designation of the burial places of Christians. The name of *catacombs*, which at Rome properly designated only the subterranean of St. Sebastian, was not employed to designate the underground Christian cemeteries in general until the ninth century.

5. *Their origin exclusively Christian.*—But where were the Christians to find space wherein to excavate the sepulchres required for their dead?

The Protestants, Burnet and Misson, reply that they availed themselves of the sand-pits which were found ready to hand, opened by the pagans for the supply of cement or other materials used in the building of the city. Else, why the name of *arenaria, crypta arenaria*, given to them by ancient authorities? Hence these writers represent the catacombs as containing pagan tombs, or, at best, tombs of Christians interred after the peace of the Church, and which afterwards became stores of sacred relics, to be sold by superstitious monks to a deluded laity. Artaud and Münter in our own day repeat this same account. Dr. Maitland,[1] however, refutes the opinion about

[1] *The Church in the Catacombs,* etc.

the pagan tombs, but defends the assertion that the catacombs were not originally excavated by Christian hands. Nor is it wonderful that he should have held this opinion in England, since Buonarotti, Boldetti, Lupi, and Bottari, defended it at Rome. It was only when Father Marchi and the brothers de Rossi commenced their patient and laborious explorations of the cemeteries themselves, that the mistake was completely cleared up. It was found that the form of the catacombs, the arrangement of the corridors, the nature of the soil traversed by them, and the marked differences between them and the still existing pagan sand-pits, all forbid the supposition that they were merely adaptations for Christian purposes of excavations originally pagan. The galleries, or corridors, are evidently made to command easy access to the tombs; long, narrow, and frequently intersecting each other at right angles, they have every quality that a passage excavated for the sole purpose of obtaining building materials ought not to have. Besides, the catacombs are excavated in a soil which supplies no materials for building. The ground about Rome presents three kinds of volcanic rocks—the *tufo litoide*, which is hard as stone and suited for building; the *tufo granulare;* and the *puzzolana*, which is employed in cement. It is observed that the soil in which the catacombs are excavated is precisely the *tufo granulare*, which alone of all these is of no use for building purposes, but, on the other hand, well adapted, by its nature, for excavations, the *litoide* being too hard, and the *puzzolana* too friable, for such a purpose. It was clearly, then, no spirit of commercial speculation that led to the formation of the catacombs. Nor does the name *arenarium*, applied to the catacombs, prove their pagan origin; for, as Michele de Rossi shows, this name was applied only to five out of the entire number, and the entrance to these five was in connection with an *arenarium*. It is impossible, however, to confound what formed part of the *arenarium* with what was excavated for the purposes of the cemetery, the passages of the former being twice, three times, or even four times wider and larger than the galleries of the latter.

But, how was it possible for the Christians, persecuted as they were, to execute a work so colossal, without attracting the attention of their relentless enemies? or, if observed, how was it permitted to them to continue their undertaking? These questions, hitherto presenting serious difficulties, have been solved by the Cavalier de Rossi.

The Roman law gave permission to every individual to construct a sepulchral monument on his own land, and to excavate a subterranean chamber for his dead, which sepulchral monument and subterranean chamber became at once religious property, sacred and inviolable. Hence wealthy Christians, and there were many such from the very beginning, had the same opportunities as those enjoyed by wealthy pagans of constructing monuments in which to bury their own deceased relatives and friends, as well as the martyrs or other faithful. A space of land, *area*, was left free around the sepulchre, and to this frequently was added a second space, *area adjecta*. This field, which was inviolable under the protection of the law, became the centre of the excavations required for the cemetery; and thus the cemetery itself came to be looked upon in the beginning as a family burial place and the private property of individuals. The architecture and ornamentation of these early cemeteries bear all the marks of the period of security under which they were designed and executed. But, in the course of time, the cemeteries became too extensive to be considered as burial places of private families. It could not be concealed any longer that they belonged to the Christian community, and this fact was well known even to the pagan magistrates. Thus it came to pass that the emperors themselves had to take up a definite position with respect to the Christian body. Some of them, it is probable, recognized them as a legally constituted community, or at least tolerated them, considering them as one of the funeral societies, *collegia funeraticia*, recognized and respected by the general law of the empire. But others of the emperors, the declared enemies of Christianity, revoked such recognitions, and we find mention in history of frequent irruptions made by the pagans into the peaceable retreats of the catacombs, and of pontiffs slain while they were celebrating the Holy Mysteries on the tombs of the martyrs, and of massacres of the faithful who were assisting at the solemn rite. In A.D. 257, the emperor Valerian forbade the Christians to assemble at their cemeteries, and in A.D. 260, Gallienus restored them to the bishops.

But whence came the enormous resources which enabled a persecuted community to excavate this subterranean city? To meet this question we should remember that the excavations were always necessarily confined to the lands belonging to Christian proprietors, since the law peremptorily prohibited all interference with the land of another. This shows that there must have been many Christians of great wealth; and the Roman Church still preserves the tradition of their riches and generosity. Besides, the Church possessed a fund formed of the monthly contributions and donations of the whole body of the faithful, and this fund not only supported the clergy, the orphans and widows, but also paid the expenses of the burial of the poor. Each cemetery was provided with a staff of

excavators, called *fossores*. Resources such as these, combined
with such an organization and uninterrupted work, will easily
explain how the infant Church was enabled to achieve so
colossal an undertaking as the subterranean Rome. We should
also bear in mind the language used by Tacitus and Pliny in
describing the immense multitude of persons of every description converted by the apostles and their early disciples.
Tertullian did not hesitate to tell the magistrates that if the
Christians should resolve to emigrate, the empire would become
a desert.

5. *Their gradual growth and subsequent abandonment.*—
From what we have said hitherto, it is plain that the growth
of the subterranean city of Rome was necessarily gradual
and slow. Hence, the several cemeteries belong to various
ages, and constitute so many successive links in the chain of
Christian antiquity. It is not possible to define with equal precision the age of them all, but the age of several out of the
whole number may be determined with a great degree of ac-
curacy. At least six (or seven, if we include that of St. Peter's
at the Vatican, destroyed to make way for the basilica) belong
to the times of the apostles, or of their earliest disciples. First
comes the cemetery called after Commodilla on the hill, the
skirt of which was removed in the construction of the basilica
over the spot where St. Paul had been buried. The oldest
inscription bearing a consular date, which has yet been found,
was found here; it is dated A.D. 107, forty years after the
death of St. Peter. Another, dated A.D. 110, was found in the
neighbourhood of the first. Next in order comes the cemetery
of Domitilla, on the Via Ardentina, which contains paintings
of the remotest antiquity, and similar in style to the paintings
which are found in the pagan sepulchres of the *Columbaria* of
the first century. The two cemeteries on the Appian Way
exhibit every mark of most ancient origin, by their coloured
stuccoes and their constructions in masonry. In the cemetery
of Priscilla also, on the *Salaria Nuova*, where Pudens, the
senator, converted by St. Peter, was buried, may be seen frescoes of the finest classic style, stuccoes, and inscriptions in
language of primitive simplicity traced in red characters.
Finally, the cemetery of St. Agnes has furnished stuccoed
crypts and inscriptions of great beauty in the style of the first
ages, although the part of the cemetery now accessible does
not go back beyond the third century.

These and other catacombs were not only resting places for
the dead, but also places of meeting for the living worshippers
of Christ. From the narrow corridors you enter wide and spa-
cious chambers, opening sometimes one into the other, and con-

31 **з**

taining episcopal chairs, altars, and various other objects employed in divine worship.

To the second century belong the cemeteries of Pretextatus,
of Maximus, etc. In the third century, small chapels, *cella me-
moriae,* began to be raised on the ground above, over the
cemeteries, which, in turn, were succeeded by larger ones, and
wide openings, called *lucernaria,* to admit light and air, were
made. The subterranean spaces were placed under the care of
priests, and thus each one of the cemeteries formed a parish,
governed in canonical form by its own clergy. When Constan-
tine restored peace to the Church, the insignificant over-ground
chapels gave way to the stately basilicas, the foundation of
which not seldom required the destruction of part of the cemetery. St. Peter's, St. Paul's, St. Laurence's, St. Agnes', and
others, are examples of the change which took place at this
period of development.

The ardent desire entertained by the faithful to repose, after
death, near the bodies of the martyrs, led them to excavate
loculi, or graves, even in the walls which had been ornamented
with frescoes. This occasioned the mutilation of many of the
paintings.

Pope Damasus (A.D. 366) who has left it written that he
did not think himself worthy of resting near the sacred ashes
of the martyrs, employed all his authority to put an end to
this custom. He inaugurated a new epoch for the catacombs.
He restored and enlarged the stairs and the *lucernaria,* and
composed poetical inscriptions which he caused to be carved
on marble in elegant characters, since known as Damasian
letters. The practice of burying the dead in the excavated
graves, or *loculi,* began from this time to fall into disuse, and
ceased altogether about the year 410, when Rome was taken
by Alaric. After that period we have no more interments in
the catacombs, which became places of pious pilgrimage for the
faithful. Many of the cemeteries which had been destroyed
by the invading barbarians, were restored. But, as the aspect
of public affairs grew more and more gloomy, and the Cam-
pagna lost its population, the devastation of the Lombards
became still more disastrous. In 756 the popes began to translate the relics of the martyrs to the city basilicas, where they
could be in greater security. Adrian the First and Leo the
Third made some efforts to save the catacombs, but, in 817,
under Paschal the First the translation of the relics recom-
menced on a still larger scale. In his reign two thousand three
hundred bodies of martyrs were translated to St. Praxedes'
church in Rome. From the middle of the ninth century the
catacombs may be said to have been abandoned. The writings

of the eleventh, twelfth, and following centuries down to the fifteenth, furnish very little information about the state of the cemeteries; and the *Itineraria* of these ages abound in topographical errors. It was only from the time of Bosie that they became known to modern science.

(*To be continued.*)

REMARKS ON THE ADDRESS PRESENTED TO THE QUEEN BY THE IRISH PROTESTANT BISHOPS.

(COMMUNICATED).

In reflecting on the great subject of political moment of the day, the public attention is forcibly attracted to the " address to the Queen of the Irish Protestant bishops". Their manner of address, the motives put forward by them, their reception by Royalty, and the answer they received, are all points of the deepest interest to the nation. Hence it is not to be wondered that friends and enemies should closely observe their manoeuvres and carefully weigh their arguments. An impartial observer cannot fail to see the singularity of their proceeding, as well as the futility of these arguments.

The Irish Establishment bishops!—the mere creatures of the state, claiming rights and privileges—what rights or what privileges can they claim except those which their founders conferred upon them? King, lords, and commons made them. Hence, king, lords, and commons can unmake them. Whence did they come? What is their origin? What is their constitution? What their professions? They are the slaves of the state, their origin is from the state. Their very constitution makes them the slaves of the state. King, or queen, lords, and commons made you: hence they can unmake you. You are earthly, not heavenly. You have hitherto gloried in your origin. The thing that is made cannot murmur against him who made it.

But only listen to their claims. They say their claims are founded on prescription " of time immemorial". The Protestant Church indeed claiming a *prescription of time immemorial.* Dr. Brady, a Protestant clergyman, will tell of their origin, and will refute by the most authentic history their assertions. Do we forget the history of the Reformation? Do we forget the confiscations, the sacrilegious usurpations of the sixteenth century? Is history ignored, or are the traditions of the nation obliterated? The memory of the Protestant usurpation of property is but of yesterday. It is fresh in the records, the annals, the traditions of our country. True, that property was devoted to sacred uses— praying for the dead, relieving the distressed, consoling the afflicted, feeding the hungry, clothing the naked, etc. Is it now devoted to these charitable objects?

" They believe there are no more precious arrangements than solemnly to set apart inviolably some portion of a nation's wealth for the service of the Almighty and the support of His ministers".

But for what ministers of religion was that portion which they now claim, set apart? Was it not for Catholic purposes? Hence, as such was *inviolable*, they are the unjust possessors of their neighbours' property. But the state gave it to them: hence the state can take it away. Yes, such a fund was in the hands of those who had no claim to it; nor would they make restitution until the instinctive honesty of the nation could no longer tolerate the injustice. The voice of reason has at length been heard, and that odious religious ascendency, which during three centuries added insult to injustice, shall be banished for ever.

What a *dissipation*, according to these advocates—although the money hitherto unjustly possessed by them will be given to feed the poor, to clothe the naked, to cure the sick and infirm; yet in their minds such a disposition of property is " dissipation". We cannot help recalling to mind the sentence to be pronounced on the day of general judgment by God Himself with regard to those works of mercy which our worthy advocates would stigmatize with the odious term of " dissipation".

But however deeply they may be affected by material losses, they are much more sensibly affected by the spiritual evils which will follow in the wake of such a measure. At the same time the measure in contemplation will not prevent them from still recognizing the sovereign of the kingdom as supreme head of their church. The contemplated measure is merely of a material kind. It will make no change in the administration or constitution of their church. Hence their complaint is unfounded. But they instinctively feel that their existence depends on earthly, material causes; because it is earthly, not heavenly. The golden chain which tied it to the state prevented it from sinking into the gulf of time in which the heresies of past ages have drifted never to appear again. If their acknowledgment of the Queen's spiritual supremacy be sincere, it must be founded on spiritual motives. Hence it should be of little moment whether they were to receive an endowment from the state or not.

Her Majesty possesses too much political wisdom to be caught by the insidious flattering insinuations of these worthy bishops. She knows too well that the brightest jewel in her crown is impartial justice to all her subjects and religious equality to all denominations. Her Majesty knows too well that the Church of Christ is not national, but universal. If they possess authority and influence, as they say they do, why should that authority and influence be transferred to another church? Is not this an acknowledgment that their church owes its existence to state patronage and state influence?

It requires no small amount of self-restraint to bear with patience their unwarrantable assumptions. Why do Catholics resent the grievance of the establishment? It is because Catholics are unjustly obliged to support a church which they disown and a religion which they abhor. Catholics say, let Protestants support their own religion as we support ours. Let not Protestant ministers or Protestant bishops enjoy any social or political influence which we do not enjoy. And in allegiance to their Queen Catholics yield not to the members of any religious denomination. For their allegiance is not based on earthly motives; it is founded on religion, the most powerful motive that can influence man. And our gracious Majesty has frequently manifested her confidence in the loyalty of her Catholic subjects. Yes, and if the day of trial were to come, which God may avert, her Majesty would not find more devoted supporters of her throne, or defenders of her august person, than her much maligned Catholic subjects.

They point out further mischiefs. "This measure will open new fountains of bitterness". Amongst whom? Surely not amongst Catholics. Nor amongst dissenters. Oh! yes, they tell us that new fountains of bitterness will arise amongst the Irish Protestants. Their loyalty will be shaken. They were kept by the loaves and fishes, and now that these are taken away they will become Fenians. This is a terrible evil indeed, but not likely to alarm the country or parliament. Loyalty so sordid is not worth the purchase. Many a tear of bitterness did that sordid loyalty wring from the heart of unhappy Catholic Ireland. May that fountain of bitterness be now closed and sealed for ever.

They next refer to some of the injustices with which the measure of disestablishment or disendowment would be fraught. They might bear forsooth with patience their own personal losses—although the public is already informed how they managed the bishops' lands, etc. But they have relatives looking forward to the same emoluments, and how can they be ignored? The sons and daughters, the sons-in-law, nephews and nieces,

et hoc genus omne. What will become of their splendid man-
sions, their sumptuous entertainments, their purple and fine
linen? Lazarus might have been allowed to lie at their gates
covered with ulcers, seeking for the crumbs that fell from the
table.

Our petitioners are now ready to renounce the great principle
of Protestantism. They say that oral teaching is essential to the
church. That the Bible and Bible alone is not and cannot be the
rule of Protestant faith. They also require sacraments. It would
be well if they could tell what sacraments they mean. Is it
Baptism? Is it the Lord's Supper? Oh! but they feel for
the richer portion of their flocks! their rights and interests.
Yes, there are few who have not some relation living on the
spoils, and how they will suffer. They have the bowels of
mercy also for the poor Protestants, who have no rich Protestant
neighbour to share with them his abundance and supply their
deficiency. But we may be allowed to ask where are the poor
Protestants to be found separated from their richer fellows?
Surely those who possess the wealth of the land may easily
make provision for their poor co-religionists.

Here again they make a profession alike unmeaning and contra-
dictory. They speak of the witness of their church. What is it?
or who are they? "which no man can usurp". How reconcile this
with the profession of the spiritual supremacy of the Queen. I
have too much respect for her gracious Majesty to say anything
derogatory to her temporal rights and privileges. Nor do I
think her Majesty supposes her Catholic faithful subjects intend
to derogate from her authority or infringe upon her privileges.

When we petition the legislature to disendow the Established
Church, we do not require Protestants to renounce the Queen's
spiritual supremacy; nor do we require of them to injure
their poorer fellow Protestants. We do not require that the Protestants would be prevented from supporting their own church.
But we require equal rights and privileges under the same constitution. If they are so confident in the perpetuity of their
church, they should fear no evil would follow its disendowment.
But through the veil we may clearly discover how little confidence they have in its perpetuity. They know Protestantism
has no other hold on its followers than the mere temporal endowments. The great motive is money. Remove this inducement,
and they will become the followers of Rome. Oh! that is the
evil. Yes, they will become the followers of a religion which
does not require the wealth of the nation to support its ministers,
nor the state to shield it under the aegis of its authority. Oh!
the "catastrophe". The day of general judgment will be acce-
lerated, for the light of the Reformation will be extinguished

for ever. They are unselfish in their address. They are zea-
lously afraid of the English and Scotch branches. They feel,
unless supported by some powerful arm, it is gone, and gone
for ever.

Their conclusion is a strange contradiction with their first profession, and far from being respectful to her Majesty. They
"are overseers"—but they should remember she is overseer
above them all. It is for her to decide, to judge, to decree; for
them to obey.

Her Majesty is too clear-sighted to receive flattery at the
expense of justice; and she is faithful to the constitution, and
will not depart from the principle to which the legislative institution of the country is bound. In her enlightened wisdom she
will deal equal-handed justice to all her faithful subjects, nor
sustain an odious religious ascendency which the united wisdom
of the nation so strongly condemns. This wisdom is more
likely to come from above than the wisdom their lordships
would pray for. Guided by this wisdom her Majesty will secure the greatest blessing a sovereign can desire—to rule her
subjects with equal justice, and thus give stability to her dy-
nasty and glory to her reign.

DOCUMENTS.

I.

*Address of the St. Peter's Pence Central Committee, Dublin, to
His Holiness, transmitting the names of the contributors to
the special Collection, 1st February, 1868.*

Beatissime Pater,

Infrascripti presbyteri Dioeceseos Dublinensis, nomine Consilii
Moderatoris Confraternitatis Sancti Petri praedictae civitatis, ad pedes
Sanctitatis Tuae provoluti, pietatem, amorem, ac summam reveren-
tiam quibus erga Sanctitatem Tuam afficimur, ea qua decet humi-
litate et devotione exprimere vehementer expetimus.

Arctissima sane illa unio, quam cum Beati Petri successore Hiber-
nica nostra gens tam firmiter constanterque semper servavit ejusdem gentis decus singulare ac summum solatium. Caeterum in
nullo historiae nostrae saeculo magis quam hisce temporibus fuit
haec unio cum supremo Ecclesiae pastore tam firma et arcta vel toties

manifestata. Cum enim octo abhinc annis ad aures nostras perve-
nerit notitia illa infausta quod homines perditissimi in principatum
Tuum civilem manus sacrilegas injecissent, quanto cordis dolore
perculsi fuimus, nulla verba satis explicare possunt. In tuis tunc
tribulationibus participes effecti sumus, in dolore tuo dolentes, cum
tuisque lachrymis lachrymas nostras permiscentes. Caput enim dole-
bat et membra eo magis ipsi compatiebantur. Pater ingemuit, et
filii fideles eo magis eum diligebant. Pastor percussus est, et oves
eo pressius circa eum sese aggregabant. Neque hic dolor tantum fuit
internus, sed et exterius sese manifestare cupiens in plura testimonia
amoris erga Sanctitatem Tuam erupit, quae licet exigua et ad
intimos animi affectus exprimendos plane insufficientia, tamen osten-
derunt nos fideles tuos Hibernos cum Sanctitate Tua intimo nexu
consociatos esse, imo pro tutela Principatus Tui civilis cum san-
guinis effusione atque vitae dispendio decertare paratos.

Huic expressioni amoris erga Sanctitatem Tuam Confraternitas
nostra supradicta suam debet originem. Cum enim primo nuntium
de sacrilego incursu in principatum Tuum civilem acceperimus,
Eminentissimus ac Reverendissimus Card. Archiepiscopus Dublinensis hanc instituit Confraternitatem cui munus esset voluntarias oblationes fidelium hujus Dioeceseos colligere, easque ad Sanctitatem
Tuam transmittere. Ab eo usque tempore permagnum hujus Socie-
tatis privilegium fuit triginta quinque millia libras sterlinas circiter
(£35,000) ad pedes Sanctitatis Tuae deponere; ex qua summa tria
millia quatuor centum librae sterlinae (in quibus sex centum octoginta
duae librae a Dioecesi Kildariensi, sexaginta autem a vicariatu
Apostolico Regionis Occidentalis Promontorii bonae Spei) paucis
abhinc mensibus collectae sunt, cum nempe tranquillitas Principatus
Tui iterum periclitabatur; hujusce ultimae collectae maximam par-
tem jam ad Sanctitatem Tuam deferri curavimus, reliquam vero
nunc per manus Reverendissimi Rectoris Collegii Hibernorum ad
pedes Sanctitatis Tuae provoluti deponimus scilicet, 200 Libras
Sterlinas.

Has caeterasque quas fecimus, vel in posterum faciemus oblationes,
precamur Te, Beatissime Pater ut acceptare digneris, non ratione
muneris ipsius quod sentimus quam sit exiguum, sed ratione amoris,
venerationis, et reverentiae quibus una cum caeteris omnibus Hiber-
nis Sanctitatem Tuam prosequimur. Maiores nostri hunc amorem
erga Cathedram Sancti Petri semper servaverunt et exhibuerunt, eun-
demque amorem Hibernos semper praestituros esse confidimus. In-
terim haud immemores praecepti quod nobis dedit gloriosissimus
noster Apostolus, Sanctus Patricius, "Sicut Christiani ita et Romani
sitis", nos Beatitudini tuae, idest Cathedrae Petri, communione consociatos esse cum Sancto Hieronymo declaramus; Te quippe Petri
successorem, totius Christiani gregis Pastorem, ac Christi in terris
Vicarium agnoscimus et veneramur.

Perquam opportunum vero nobis videtur nomina eorum adjecto
libello exhibere, qui hac occasione in hoc exiguo amoris, et venerationis erga Sanctam Sedem testimonio praestando convenerunt.

Denique ad pedes Sanctitatis Tuae provoluti, pro Eminentissimo ac Reverendissimo Confraternitatis patrono, pro omnibus ejusdem Confraternitatis sociis et pro nobis praesertim vero pro fidelibus quorum nomina in libello exhib ntur, ac pro eorundem familiis Apostolicam benedictionem humiliter imploramus.

Datum Dublini, in die festo S. Brigidae, 1868.

PATRITIUS F. MORAN,
GUILLELMUS PURCELL, } SECRETARII.
THOMAS J. O'REILLY,

II.

Letter of our Most Holy Father to the President and Secretaries of the Peter's Pence Association, in reply to the above Address.

" Pius Papa IX.

" Dilecti Filii, salutem et Apostolicam Benedictionem. Hiberniae vestrae fides et religio commendatae semper, clarius etiam enituerunt inter adversa aliquot ab hinc saeculis, sicut aurum quod igne probatur. Per haec vero prostrema tempora novo quoque fulgore splendescere visae sunt, dum, hac Sancta Sede fraude et armis impetitâ, alii e vestratibus patriam deseruere sponte convolaturi ad Nos, et sanguinem daturi pro Ecclesiae causa; alii vero, utut annonae rerumque omnium difficultate pressi, stipem liberaliter contulere suam, in jurium Nostrorum defensionem et inopiae Nobis factae levamen. Id autem acceptissimam Nobis fecit adjectam amantissimis litteris vestris eorum nominum syllogem, uti nobile religionis vestrae ac filialis in Nos pietatis monumentum, novumque patriae vestrae decus. Ipsis itaque, grati animi sensu perciti, uberem coelestium munerum copiam, omniaque simul necessaria subs dia adprecamur, sodalitati autem vestrae nova semper gratiarum et propagationis incrementa. Horum vero auspicem, et paternae benevolentiae Nostrae testem, Apostolicam Benedictionem Vobis universis peramanter impertimus.

" Datum Romae apud S. Petrum, die 29 Aprilis, 1868, Pontificatus Nostri anno vigesimo-secundo.

"PIUS PAPA IX.

" Dilectis Filiis,
" Rectori et Secretariis Sodalitatis Sancti Petri, Dublinum".

III.

Letter of the Cardinal Prefect of Propaganda to the Cardinal Archbishop of Dublin, on Mixed Schools.

EMINENTISSIMO E REVERENDISSIMO SIGNORE MIO OSSMO.,

La erezione di Scuole e Convitti misti di Cattolici ed Eterodossi, che da qualche tempo sventuratamente si va rendendo ogni giorno più comune, ha indotto la S. Sede, desiderosa di provvedere alla sana istruzione dei fedeli, a richiamare in proposito i giusti principii, dare le opportune regole, e porgere i necessarii avvertimenti sia per organo del S. Offizio, che della S. C. di Propaganda, secondo i casi che alla medesima sonosi denunciati. Nel presente foglio si è creduto conveniente di redigerne un compendio.

Sebbene siavi differenza tra le scuole Protestanti e Scismatiche, e generalmente parlando maggiori forse siano i danni che hanno a temersi dalle prime, pur tuttavia non lasciano anche le seconde di essere grandemente pericolose per la gioventù cattolica. Onde con circolare dei 20 Marzo 1865 la S. Congregazione di Propaganda mentre rendeva avvertiti i Vescovi Orientali del gravissimo pericolo, al quale sono esposti i giovinetti cattolici nel frequentare le anzidette scuole dirette dagli Scismatici e Protestanti, che vanno aprendosi, or più che in altra epoca nelle principali città dell' Oriente; ne eccitava altresi lo zelo ad impedire energicamente siffatta costumanza, impiegando anche all' uopo tutto il nerbo della loro ecclesiastica autorità. Ai Vescovi principalmente ed ai Parrochi incombe l' obbligo di usare le più solerti ed efficaci cure, onde persuadere i padri di famiglia non poter far essi cosa più pregiudizievole alla loro prole, alla patria ed alla nostra santa Religione, che coll' esporre i proprî figli ad un così manifesto pericolo, che sarebbe anche maggiore, qualora le scuole medesime fossero istituite col diretto intendimento di far proseliti all' eresia ed allo scisma. Ognun conosce quanta forza eserciti sull' animo giovanile l' autorità dei precettori, e come potentemente lo induca ad approvar tuttociò che in essi scorge, e da essi ascolta. Quindi avviene che in un coll' insegnamento contragga senza quasi avvertirlo i loro errori, e concepisca disprezzo della Religione cattolica. A ciò si aggiunga il giornaliero e familiare tratto coi giovani Protestanti e Scismatici, i cui costumi sovente corrotti, la indocilità, il mordace parlare contro la nostra santa Religione e contro le pratiche della Chiesa pervertono la mente, e corrompono il cuore dei condiscepoli cattolici. Nè si creda già che da ogni pericolo vadano immuni quelle fra le anzidette scuole, il cui insegnamento riguarda la elementare istituzione, ovvero materie meramente profane; imperocchè oltre ai medesimi pericoli ch' esse presentano pel consorzio e familiarità coi condiscepoli educati nella eresia e nello scisma, porgono altresì ai precettori il mezzo d' ingannare la giovanile semplicità con arti quanto meno apprese altrettanto più efficaci. Tuttociò trovasi trattato in una recente analoga istruzione emessa dalla Suprema Congregazione del S. Officio per la Svizzera sotto il giorno 26 Marzo 1866.

Si è discorso fin qui dei giovani cattolici che frequentano le scuole Protestanti e Scismatiche. Passando ora a parlare dei giovani Scismatici e Protestanti che frequentano le scuole cattoliche, egli è chiaro che in questo secondo caso non esistono pei giovani cattolici tutti quei pericoli, che si dissero concorrere nel caso precedente: imperocchè essendo cattolico il precettore, cattolici gl' insegnamenti e i libri, nulla v' ha a temere da questo lato. Ed e perciò che questa S. Congregazione di Propaganda si è mostrata altre volte indulgente a tollerare o anche ad ammettere che nelle scuole cattoliche istituite nelle Missioni e dirette dai Missionarî si ricevessero ed ammaestrassero dai precettori cattolici anche gli eterodossi. Non disconosceva però la stessa S. Congregazione che anche in tali scuole per direzione e per insegnamento cattoliche non mancherebbe qualche grave pericolo per l' ammissione dei detti giovani Scismatici e Protestanti a motivo principalmente del quotidiano contatto che questi avrebbero coi figli dei Cattolici. Laonde nel permettere tale promiscuità fu sollecita di prescrivere alcune cautele necessarie specialmente a rimuovere dai giovanetti Cattolici il pericolo di perversione, come pure dagli acattolici il pericolo d' indifferentismo. Gioverà indicare talune risoluzioni prese in proposito da questa S. Congregazione. Una particolare adunanza tenutasi ai 18 Decembre 1742 fu di avviso potersi permettere ai Missionarî Cappuccini di Moscovia che oltre alle scuole di lingue straniere e di scienze indifferenti, che allora si tenevano pei soli figli dei Cattolici, altre ne potessero tenere per tutti gli acattolici che volessero concorrervi, destinando all' uopo una camera separata. Certamente la separazione di camera elimina o almeno rende assai rimoti gli anzidetti pericoli che nascono dalla promiscuità di giovani Cattolici ed acattolici, e che formano appunto la principale difficoltà delle scuole miste, se pure possano dirsi propriamente tali nel caso che si assegni luogo distinto e separato ai discepoli eterodossi. Un tal metodo però di separazione assai difficilmente potrebbe adottarsi ovunque sì per mancanza di locale e di mezzi, come pure per la esigenza di più maestri, di cui havvi ordinariamente scarsezza nei luoghi di Missione.

Sul finire dello scorso secolo i Padri Riformati Missionarî nell' Egitto superiore aveano aperto delle scuole in varie stazioni di quella Missione pei giovanetti Cattolici, e ad esse concorrevano ancora i figli dei Copti scismatici. La Congregazione generale adunatasi ai 29 Agosto dell' anno 1791 opinò potersi ciò tollerare per allettare gli eretici Copti al cattolicismo e non irritarli, aggiungenda però che " periculum perversionis per magistrorum diligentiam removeatur". Analogamente a questa risoluzione del S. Consesso fu scritto al Prefetto di quella Missione, non doversi far difficoltà che i figli degli eretici vadano alle scuole Cattoliche. Ma che siccome talvolta qualche giovanetto discolo eretico potrebbe pervertire alcuno dei cattolici, però i maestri debbano avere di ciò cura e non ammettere nelle scuole i giovanetti eretici licenziosi. All' opposto moltissimo bene si deve sperare dalla frequenza degli eretici alle scuole Cattoliche, potendosi così imbevere dei sodi principî della nostra vera Religione, e potendo i maestri insinuarsi nel loro spirito per guadagnarli alla Chiesa.

Omettendo altre consimili risoluzioni giova riferire come nell' anno 1853 i Vescovi Armeni della provincia ecclesiastica di Costantinopoli riuniti in conferenze avendo annoverato fra i mezzi opportuni per la conversione degli scismatici nazionali anche quello di dare accesso ai loro figli alle scuole Cattoliche, la Congregazione generale di Propaganda ordinò si scrivesse all' Arcivescovo Primate significandogli che il mezzo proposto ravvisavasi molto acconcio a procurare la conversione degli scismatici, ma si richiedeva però un metodo assai prudenziale per non far nascere degli inconvenienti; che due sono i pericoli che possono derivarne, il primo che i giovani Scismatici pervertano i giovanetti Cattolici, se non si prendono tutte le cautele per impedire che parlino a lungo fra loro. Imperrochè avvenendo naturalmente che fra gli Scismatici sianvi dei giovani astuti, di talento, radicati nello scisma in forza della domestica educazione, e che tra gli allievi Cattolici ve ne siano alcuni di scarso talento e di poco sentimento religioso, facilmente i primi pervertirebbero i secondi. L'altro pericolo è di rendere ipocriti i giovanetti Scismatici, se venissero obbligati ad intervenire agli esercizî religiosi, al pari dei figli de' Cattolici, perchè in tale caso vi sarebbe pericolo che simulassero la professione del cattolicismo contro la erronea loro conscienza; e si renderebbero proclivi all'indifferentismo. Si avvertì poi lo stesso Monsig. Arcivescovo che non s'intendeva parlare di ammetterli ai Sagramenti, perche in tal caso dovrebbe precedere la formale abiura, e la sincera dichiarazione di ritornare alla religione Cattolica. Per ultimo s'insinuò ai Vescovi dell' anzidetta provincia, che per tener lontani tali pericoli dalle scuole, in cui insieme ai giovanetti Cattolici, ricevonsi anche gli Scismatici, allorquando si riunirebbero in Concilio Provinciale formassero un apposito regolamento per siffatte scuole miste da sottoporsi all' approvazione di questa S. Congregazione.

Resta finalmente a dirsi qualche cosa intorno all' ammissione dei giovani Scismatici e Protestanti nei pensionati e convitti Cattolici. Non potrebbe però darsi una norma adeguata e sicura applicabile a ciascun collegio, convitto o pensionato senza aver prima particolari ed accuratissime notizie sopra tutte quelle circostanze, dalla cui cognizione dipende appunto il giudizio che deva portarsi sull' anzidetta promiscua convivenza di Cattolici ed Eterodossi. Sarebbe quindi necessaria di conoscere il preciso scopo dei convitti, la condizione e l' età di quelli che vi si ammettono, la qualità e il grado d' istruzione che vi si dà, il regolamento onde è ordinata l' interna disciplina, specialmente per ciò che spetta alle relazioni le quali passano fra i fanciulli (o fanciulle se trattisi di convitto di sesso femminile) di diverso culto; se possano liberamente trattare e parlare tra loro, se sia ad essi proibito di ragionare intorno a punti religiosi. Altro articolo assai necessario a conoscersi è il modo, con cui gli acattolici vengono diretti in materia di religione, vale a dire se vengono educati nella religione Cattolica con o senza il consenso dei genitori; qualora non sono educati cattolicamente, se è dato loro il permesso, od anche imposto l' obbligo di assistere in un coi Cattolici alla S. Messa ed alle pratiche di pietà, se debbono astenersi sempre dal riceverli qualche volta nelle loro chiese Scismatiche, e chi ve li accompagni. Interessa ancora sapere quale sia in ciascun convitto il numero dei Protestanti e Scismatici e in quale proporzione si trovi con quello dei Cattolici.

Occorrerebbe pertanto che i Superiori delle verre Missioni si procurassere possibilmente e rimettessero alla S. C. le suaccennate

Documents. 467

notizie intorno a quei convitti misti che si trovassero dipendenti
dalla loro giurisdizione per quindi riceverne le analoghe instruzioni
adattate alle peculiari circostanze di ciascuno di essi. Frattanto però
non sarà del tutto inutile riferire una risoluzione emessa recente-
mente dal S. Offizio pel caso di un convitto misto di giovanette Cattoliche di rito Latino, e di Scismatiche di rito Orientale. Pria però
di esporla fa d'uopo dare un cenno dell'interno regolamento del
convitto medesimo, sensa di che non protrebbe ben comprendersi la
portata dell'anzidetta risoluzione. Nello stesso stabilmento diretto
da Religiose in un colle giovannette Cattoliche vengono educate
anche le Scismatiche di rito Orientale. La proporzione del numero
fra le une e le altre non fu sempre la medesima; da cinque anni
però a questa parte le Scismatiche costituiscono presso a poco la
terza parte dell'educandato, e vengono esse instituite non solamente
nelle scienze profane, ma eziandio nella religione Cattolica, quante
volte i lori genitori Scismatici ne faciano espressa richiesta. Oltre
alla istituzione Cattolica le ridette educande Scismatiche hanno in
commune colle Cattoliche pie lezioni, esercizî spirituali, ed assistono
con esse quotidianamente alla S. Messa. In addietro pregavano
anche insieme, ma presentemente per disposizione dell'Ordinario
onde evitare la communicazione *in divinis*, pregano separatamente
dalle Cattoliche di rito Latino le une e le altre nella loro lingua
nazionale. Presso dimanda dei genitori le giovanette Scismatiche una
o due volte all'anno sono condotte sotto la vigilanza di persona di
fiducia alla chiesa Scismatica per ricevere i Sagramenti, le altre si
astengono dal frequentarle. E da notarsi che gli Ordinarî diocesani
pro tempore non approvarono mai il metodo finora descritto, che si
osserva nel suaccennato convitto, ma lo tollerarono per la speranza che
le fanciulle educate cattolicamente tornate alle loro case e divenute
sui iuris abbraccerebbero la religione Cattolica, vi condurrebbero i
propri mariti e vi educherebbero la prole, come di fatti già dieci di
esse abiurarono lo scisma, ed una converti il suo marito; e quand'
anche non tutte si convertano, tuttavia speravano quei Prelati, che la
educazione ricevuta cattolicamente farebbe loro deporre i pregiudizi
contro la Chiesa Cattolica, l'odio ed il disprezzo contro i Cattolici;
nè d'altra parte vi è a temere, come assicurava l'attuale Ordinario
diocesano, che le giovanette materialmente Scismatiche, addivengano
tali formalmente, atteso il tardo loro ingegno, secondo che attestano
i Superiorori del rimentovato stabilimento, il quale d'altronde se
non ammettesse le giovanette Scismatiche, mancherebbe dei mezzi
sufficienti per mantenere le Religiose che lo diriggono, e non si
troverebbe in grado di diminuire la retta alle convittrici latine d'
ordinario povere e bisognose.

Presso tale relazione la Suprema Congregazione del S. Offizio
rispose come siegue.

Feria VI loco IV die 1 Iunii 1866.

"Tolerari posse ut puellae schismaticae in collegium admittantur
quod Sorores dirigunt, dummodo bonam praeseferaut indolem, iuxta

exposita instituantur, nec tamen obligentur ad assistendum Missae
Sacrificio aliisque functionibus ecclesiasticis, verum id earum arbitrio
relinquatur, vetito quidem ne umquam disputationes cum puellis
catholicis habeant de rebus ad religionem spectantibus; ne templum
adeant schismaticum a ministris schismaticis sacramenta recepturae;
quod si in aliquo casu id impediri nullo modo possit Sorores passive
se habeant, et pariter vetito, ne puellae ab amicis et coniunctis, ex-
ceptis parentibus et tutoribus, absque licentia Ordinari visitentur; de
quibus omnibus clare et explicite instructi fiant, et in iis consentiant
parentes vel tutores earumdem puellarum, antequam ipsae ad collegium admittantur. Idque scribatur R. P. D. Archiepiscopo (Ordinario) cum advertentia ut curet omnium horum executionem, et
bonum spirituale puellarum quoad fieri poterit, etiam post egressum
e collegio, et instruantur Sorores quod si aliqua ad fidem catholicam
converti petat, res ad ipsum Archiepiscopum erit deferenda, qui
iuxta casus adiuncta prudenter providebit, et sedulo caveat ne ex
admissione schismaticarum ullum ne minimvm quidem perversionis
vel indifferentismi periculum puellis Catholicis subsit".

(To be continued.)

NOTICE OF BOOK.

Notes on the Rubries of the Roman Ritual, regarding the sacraments in general, Baptism, the Eucharist, and Extreme
Unction, by the Rev. James O'Kane, Senior Dean, St.
Patrick's College, Maynooth. Second edition, Duffy, Dublin,
1868, pp. 527.

This second edition of Rev. James O'Kane's *Notes on the
Rubries* comes before us with a *Prologus Galeatus* in the shape
of an important Decree of the Sacred Congregation of Rites,
which declares the work to be a *vere commendabile et accura-
tissimum opus.* This is high praise indeed, and coming from
such a quarter, leaves nothing to be added by us. The Sacred
Congregation of Rites draws attention to four passages in the
first edition, and directs some changes to be made therein. It
is unnecessary to say that these directions have been accurately
carried out. With the exception of these four passages, of one
other change made in consequence of a late decision (n. 699),
and of the addition of a foot-note and an instruction, the
second edition is an exact reprint of the first It is highly
creditable to the author that his work, entering, as it does,
into such minute and detailed particulars on a very wide range
of subjects, upon which so many rules have been issued, should
have passed through the searching examination of the Congregation of Rites, and received the approbation of that body.

THE CONFRATERNITY OF ST. PETER.

Ever since the year 1859, the enemies of the Church, and enemies of the Holy Father, as *Head of the Church*, have exerted themselves with unceasing energy to destroy the temporal power of the Pope; and they have pursued their object in a far more systematic manner than at any previous period. The deep purpose and design which they had, and still have, in view, are sufficiently clear. It is not that they are in love with the Piedmontese rule; neither is it a desire to swell the fame of Victor Emmanuel or to enrich his treasury that actuates them. The Infidel and Protestant parties throughout Europe have *one* purpose in view, and it is *this*:—they do not or will not believe in the Divine Mission of the Church, or the Divine influence by which it is upheld; and they hate its authority, its morality, and the restraints which its inspired teaching places upon their corrupt inclinations, weak but vain judgments, and self-will.

Their *pride of intellect* causes them to hate it in theory, their *corrupt nature* makes them detest it in practice; and both combine to unite them together, one and all, in perpetual opposition to a Church that will not compromise truth. The first means they have recourse to to accomplish its destruction, is calumny; the second is spoliation and fraud. They think that by assailing its Head, and the centre of its organization, they may interrupt the wonderful machinery by which it has pleased Providence that the Vicar of Christ should teach and govern the Church in our time. Their plan could not have been better devised; although it could never succeed, for we know that God will uphold his Church, whatever happens. But we must bear in mind that it is our duty not to look to a supernatural interposition of Providence to obtain that which we ourselves, by using proper exertions, can accomplish.

If we stand by, and see with calm indifference the Holy Father plundered of all those human means by which he is enabled to carry on the government of the Church throughout the world, Providence will no doubt miraculously interpose to sustain His Church; but such a result could scarcely bring a blessing to those cold-hearted and selfish Catholics whose neglect of duty rendered such interposition necessary.

There is one thing which we may learn from the enemies of our Holy Father. *They are all united* in attacking him; *let us all unite* to defend him. There are some Catholics, even in our own devoted island, who are at this moment standing idly by, watching events as they roll on, just as though the interests of the Church, and the interests of the Head of the Church, were no concern of theirs. They receive all from the Church, their hopes of salvation are through that pure faith which comes to them from the Church, and they will give nothing in return. Let us hope that it is want of due consideration, rather than want of will, which keeps them thus inactive.

Since 1860, a Society (since erected into a *Confraternity*) has existed in Ireland, having for its object to unite all Catholics together in defence of the Holy Father. It has made considerable progress in several dioceses, and has assisted to supply the wants of the Holy Father by reviving the institution of "Peter's Pence". It is regarded with pleasure and affection by the Holy Father. The eminent prelate who rules this see has given to it his earnest coöperation and the sanction of his high authority; and it was especially dear to the deceased Primate, whose loss all the Catholics of our island so sincerely deplore.

It is called the "Confraternity of St. Peter".

Its objects are threefold.

Firstly, *the diffusion of sound Catholic principles.*

Secondly, *the promotion of prayers for the Church.*

Thirdly, *the voluntary offering of a small fixed sum to the Holy Father, as Peter's Pence*".

• The usual offering is *one penny*, either weekly or monthly. Every new member upon entering the Confraternity is supposed to have the intention, *at least* of making some such offering periodically; but should he be unable to continue to do so regularly, although having the intention, and continue to carry out the other two objects of the Confraternity, he remains as much a member as though he contributed. Where a *Confraternity* already exists in a parish, the only formality upon being enrolled consists of having the new member's name entered in a book kept for the purpose, with the amount of his offering opposite to it. Where no *Confraternity* exists, the new member can, upon communicating his name to one of the Council, or to a *Confraternity* in any other parish or diocese, be enrolled there. It is to be hoped that every Catholic in our island will give his name to this Confraternity. No objection can be raised upon the score of poverty, for who is there that could not afford *a penny a month?* And if there are some who cannot afford to contribute at all, who is there so poor that he cannot at least offer up a prayer? Every Catholic must answer these questions to the satisfaction of his own conscience, for the present time is one in which the Vicar of Christ may say with his Divine Master, " He that is not with me is against me".

This Confraternity is enriched with many special Indulgences, of which the following are the principal heads :—

1. A Plenary Indulgence to all the members of the Confraternity on the day on which they connect themselves with it, provided they make a good confession and communion.

2. On the Feast of SS. Peter and Paul (29th June), on the Feast of St. Peter's Chair in Rome (18th January), and on the Feast of St. Peter's Chains (1st August), a Plenary Indulgence is granted to all members of the Confraternity, who, being truly penitent, and having made a good confession and communion, shall visit a public church, and there piously pray for the concord of Christian princes, the extirpation of heresy, and the exaltation of our Holy Mother the Church.

3. An Indulgence of seven years and as many quarantines is granted to all the faithful of Christ belonging to the Confraternity, who on any day shall recite the " Lord's Prayer", the " Hail Mary", the " Glory be to the Father", etc., and the " Apostles' Creed", at least with a contrite heart.

4. An Indulgence of three hundred days is granted to the faithful belonging to the Confraternity, each time they make any donation to its funds, or perform any similar work of piety.

5. All the aforesaid Indulgences are applicable, by way of suffrage, to the souls of the faithful who have departed this life united in charity with God.

The collections made by the local Committees may be transmitted to any of those whose names are subjoined :—

PRESIDENT:

HIS EMINENCE PAUL CARDINAL CULLEN.

VICE-PRESIDENTS:

VERY REV. MONSIGNOR MEAGHER, V.G., RATHMINES.
VERY REV. MONSIGNOR FORDE, V.G., BOOTERSTOWN.
VERY REV. DR. M'CABE, V.G., KINGSTOWN.

TREASURERS:

HIS EMINENCE THE CARDINAL ARCHBISHOP.
VERY REV. MONSIGNOR O'CONNELL, DEAN, P.P.
RIGHT HON. RICHARD M. O'FERRALL.

HONORARY SECRETARIES.

VERY REV. MONSIGNOR MORAN, 55 ECCLES STREET.
REV. W. PURCELL, C.C., MARLBOROUGH STREET.
REV. THOMAS O'REILLY,   Do.